THE
DREAM
GIVER

BRUCE
WILKINSON

WITH DAVID & HEATHER KOPP

Multnomah® Publishers *Sisters, Oregon*

THE DREAM GIVER
published by Multnomah Publishers, Inc.

© 2003 by Ovation Foundation, Inc.
International Standard Book Number: 1-59052-201-X

Interior images by Steve Gardner, His Image PixelWorks

Scripture quotations are from:
The Holy Bible, New King James Version © 1984 by Thomas Nelson, Inc.

Multnomah is a trademark of Multnomah Publishers, Inc.,
and is registered in the U.S. Patent and Trademark Office.
The colophon is a trademark of Multnomah Publishers, Inc.

Printed in the United States of America

For information:
MULTNOMAH PUBLISHERS, INC.
POST OFFICE BOX 1720
SISTERS, OREGON 97759

04 05 06 07 08 -DI- 10 9 8 7 6 5

CONTENTS

PART II
THE JOURNEY TO YOUR BIG DREAM

This book is for anyone who has ever hoped
or believed they could achieve something
remarkable with their lives.

David and Heather Kopp have been a vital
part of creating this book.
Their commitment, skill, and encouragement
have been a deep inspiration.
Thank you, my good friends,
for being Champions to this Dreamer.

Most of all, I wish to acknowledge the Dream Giver Himself.
For without Him, none of us would have a compelling
Dream to trade our lives for.

PREFACE

*D*o you believe every person on earth was born with a dream for his or her life?

No matter where I travel in the world—whether among hard-charging Manhattan urbanites or villagers in southern Africa—I have yet to find a person who *didn't* have a dream. They may not be able to describe it. They may have forgotten it. They may no longer believe in it.

But it's there.

I call this universal and powerful longing a Big Dream. Like the genetic code that describes your unique passions and abilities, your Big Dream has been woven into your being from birth. You're the only person with a Dream quite like yours.

And you have it for a reason: to draw you toward the kind of life you were born to love!

Welcome to my new book, *The Dream Giver*, a practical and innovative guide to achieving your Big Dream.

The Dream Giver is made up of two parts.

Part 1 is "The Parable of the Dream Giver." This is the story of Ordinary, a Nobody who leaves the Land of Familiar to pursue his Big Dream. The parable follows Ordinary on the journey to his Dream. This story will introduce you to the big ideas I want to talk about in the next section.

Part 2 is called "The Journey to Your Big Dream." I will serve as your Dream Coach in these pages, helping you to problem-solve and to reach for important personal breakthroughs. This section is designed to inspire you along the journey toward your Dream. For even more help, I invite you to visit www.TheDreamGiver.com, where you will find creative, interactive solutions for people pursuing their Dream.

In choosing a parable to teach about Dreams, I seek to follow in a long and honored tradition of conveying important life principles through a simple story. C. S. Lewis and *The Chronicles of Narnia*, for example. Or John Bunyan and *Pilgrim's Progress*. And who can forget the parables of the Good Samaritan and the Prodigal Son? For communicating truth to people of all times and cultures, the parable just may be the most powerful teaching tool available.

If you read *The Prayer of Jabez*, you met a little-known Old Testament man who refused to settle for less. He desperately wanted to break out of the confining circumstances and expectations he had been born into. So he cried out to God for blessing, for larger borders, and for the power and protection to go with them. And God said yes.

If you pray like that, your life will change. God will expand your borders. He will move your life in a direction where you can thrive, but also where you'll face greater challenges than you've ever faced before.

In this book, I call this direction His Dream for you.

Every Dreamer soon learns that the road to the future you really want is clogged with Dream-threatening obstacles. That's why so many turn back. But what many don't realize—and what I missed for years—is that each obstacle is also an important *opportunity*. The obstacles come in a predictable sequence, and each for a very promising reason.

The better you understand the journey to your Dream and what God is doing in your life, the less likely you are to abandon your Dream.

So let me ask: Did you have a dream as a child that you lost along the way? Do you have a dream right now that seems impossible to pursue? Do you feel like God forgot to even give you a Big Dream? Or are you pursuing your dream, but experiencing setback after setback?

If your answer to any of these questions is yes, then this book is for you! Please join me for the journey of your life.

May your heart sing as you embrace what you were
created to be and do.

Warmly,

Bruce Wilkinson

Johannesburg, South Africa

THE
PARABLE
OF THE
DREAM GIVER

CHAPTER ONE

ORDINARY EMBRACES
HIS BIG DREAM

*N*ot long ago and not far away, a Nobody named
Ordinary lived in the Land of Familiar.

Every day was pretty much the same for Ordinary. In
the mornings he got up and went to his Usual Job. After
work, he ate almost the same dinner he'd eaten the
evening before. Then he sat in his recliner and watched
the box that mesmerized most Nobodies on most nights.

Sometimes, Best Friend came over to join Ordinary
in front of the box. Sometimes, Ordinary went to his
Parents' and they watched together.

For the most part, not much happened in Familiar
that hadn't happened before. Ordinary thought he was
content. He found the routines reliable. He blended in
with the crowd. And mostly, he wanted only what he had.

Until the day Ordinary noticed a small, nagging

feeling that something big was missing from his life. Or maybe the feeling was that *he* was missing from something big. He wasn't sure.

The little feeling grew. And even though Nobodies in Familiar didn't generally expect the unexpected, Ordinary began to wish for it.

◦∽◦

Time passed. Then one morning Ordinary woke up with these words echoing in his mind: *What you're missing, you already have...*

Could it be? Ordinary looked and looked. And then he discovered that in a small corner of his heart lay a Big Dream. The Big Dream told him that he, a Nobody, was made to be a Somebody and destined to achieve Great Things.

Jumping out of bed, Ordinary discovered something else—a long white feather resting on the sill of his window. Where did it come from? What did it mean? With a jolt of excitement, Ordinary decided he'd been visited by the Dream Giver.

Now, Ordinary had heard rumors of various Nobodies in Familiar waking up to a Big Dream. But he had never imagined that it could happen to him.

He rushed to get dressed, his Big Dream beating brightly in his chest. He couldn't wait to get to his Usual Job and tell Best Friend the news.

But on his way to work, Ordinary realized he had a problem. His Big Dream was *too* big for a Nobody like

Ordinary. He would be embarrassed to tell anyone. Even Best Friend would probably laugh.

Still, Ordinary was too excited to keep his dream to himself. As soon as he saw Best Friend, he blurted out the news: "The Dream Giver gave me a Big Dream! I was made to be a Somebody and destined to achieve Great Things!"

Best Friend looked surprised, but he didn't laugh. "That's very...*big*," he said. "But if I were you, I wouldn't talk about this Dream of yours too much. Nobodies around here might take you for a fool."

Ordinary didn't want to look like a fool. So after that he kept his Big Dream to himself.

Day after day, Ordinary showed up at his Usual Job. But while he worked, he thought about his Dream. He thought about how wonderful it would be to do what he loved to do instead of just dreaming about it.

Ordinary's longing for his Big Dream grew and grew, until finally he realized that he'd never be happy unless he could pursue it. Why didn't the Dream Giver make it possible?

If the Dream Giver didn't, how could Ordinary ever leave Familiar? He had payments and expenses. He had regular duties. A lot of Nobodies counted on him for a lot of things.

Ordinary felt completely stuck. Time passed, but nothing changed.

He began to hate his Usual Job. *This isn't what I was made to do,* he'd say to himself. *I just know it!*

After a while, he began to worry that maybe he hadn't received a Big Dream after all. Maybe he'd just made it all up.

And he grew sadder by the day.

One evening after work, Ordinary went to his Parents' to watch the box. But their box was broken, so the house was very quiet. It was even more quiet because his Mother was out shopping at Familiar Foods.

In the quietness, Ordinary started to think about his Dream again. He looked over at his Father sitting in his recliner, staring at the single page of *Nobody's News.* Maybe *he* could help.

"Father," said Ordinary, "I'm growing sadder by the day. I don't like my Usual Job anymore. In fact, I think I hate it."

Father looked up. "That's terrible!" he said. "What happened?"

Before he could stop himself, Ordinary started talking about the Dream Giver, and about his Big Dream. "I was made to be a Somebody and achieve Great Things!" he said. And then he told his Father the Name of his Dream. As he spoke, his voice trembled. He was sure that his Father would laugh or call him a fool.

But his Father didn't. "I'm not surprised to hear you say these things," he said.

"You're not?" said Ordinary.

"No," his Father said. "You've had that Dream ever since you were little. Don't you remember? You used to build that same dream with sticks and mud in front of this very house."

Then Ordinary *did* remember. He'd *always* had his Dream! It was what he'd always wanted to do, and what he'd always thought he'd be good at doing.

His eyes filled with tears. "Father," he said, "I think I was *born* to do this."

Ordinary and his Father sat together quietly. His Father seemed to be remembering something, too. After a while he asked, "When you woke up to your Big Dream, Son, did you happen to find...a feather?"

Ordinary was shocked. "How did you know?" he asked.

"A long time ago, I woke up to a Dream, too," his Father said. "And it came with a long white feather. It was a wonderful Dream. I kept the feather on my windowsill while I waited for a chance to pursue it. I waited and waited. But it never seemed possible... One day I noticed the feather had turned to dust."

Of all the sad words Ordinary had ever heard, these were the saddest.

Before he left that night, his Father hugged him. "Don't make the same mistake I did, Son," he said. "You don't have to stay a Nobody. You can be a Dreamer!"

❧

When Ordinary got home, he went straight to the
window and picked up the long white feather. He turned
it over carefully in his hands. He thought about his Father
and the Dream he'd left behind.

Then he had a surprising idea. Could it be that maybe
the Dream Giver gave *every* Nobody a Dream, but only
some embraced their dreams? And even fewer pursued
them?

The more he thought about it, the more he thought it
had to be true.

One thing Ordinary did know for sure: He didn't
want to repeat his Father's mistake. He wouldn't waste
another day waiting for his Dream to seem possible. He
would find a way to pursue it.

❧

Time passed. Ordinary worked hard on his plan to begin
his Dream. He made hard choices. He made difficult
changes. He even made big sacrifices.

Finally, one morning, he was ready.

Ordinary ran all the way to his Usual Job, his Dream
pounding hard in his chest. As soon as he saw Best
Friend, Ordinary blurted out the news: "That Big Dream
I told you about—I've decided to pursue it!"

Best Friend looked concerned. "You know as well as
I do that Nobodies who pursue their Dreams leave
Familiar," he said. "They set off like fools into the

Unknown, in search of a place where—"

"Yes, yes, I know," Ordinary broke in, "and I can't wait to get started!"

"But Ordinary, that journey is anything but sensible or safe. Why leave Familiar? It's so comfortable here. And besides, you've *always* lived here."

"I've thought about all that, too," said Ordinary. "But my Big Dream is too important and too wonderful to miss."

Best Friend shook his head. "So you're going to become a Dreamer," he said.

"I *am* a Dreamer!" answered Ordinary. "Today I'm going to tell my Boss that I'm leaving my Usual Job. Tomorrow I will begin my journey. Hey, Best Friend," added Ordinary eagerly, "you can have my recliner and my box!"

And with that, Ordinary walked away, humming a tune that he'd never heard before.

The night before he left Familiar...

Ordinary decided to use the long white feather to help him remember the Truth. He pulled out a notebook and wrote "My Dream Journal" on the cover. Then he dipped the quill in permanent ink, and wrote on the first page:

- The Dream Giver gave me a Big Dream before I was even born. I just finally woke up to it!

- My Dream is what I do best and what I most love to do. How could I have missed it for so long?

- I had to sacrifice and make big changes to pursue my Dream. But it will be worth it.

- It makes me sad to think that so many Nobodies are missing something so Big.

CHAPTER TWO

ORDINARY LEAVES
HIS COMFORT ZONE

*T*he next morning, Ordinary woke up at the usual
time. But instead of reporting to his Usual Job, he
packed his suitcase with the usual stuff. Then he added his
journal and a bottle of permanent ink. Just before he closed
the latch, he carefully placed his long white feather inside.

Soon, Ordinary was walking away from the
comfortable center of Familiar, where almost every
Nobody lived. He was heading toward the Border, where
almost no Nobodies ever went.

Ordinary had never dared to walk this way before.
But, like every Nobody, he knew that the farther you
walked from the center of Familiar, the less familiar
things became. He also knew that most Nobodies who
tried to leave the Comfort Zone of Familiar became so
uncomfortable, they turned around and went home.

Some were so glad to be back, they sat in their

recliner for days, waiting for nothing to happen and sighing with relief.

But Ordinary told himself he was different from most Nobodies. He would pursue his Dream, no matter what.

Brimming with anticipation, Ordinary whistled his new tune while he walked, and he dreamed about the Great Things he would accomplish. Life had never seemed so promising.

Ordinary hadn't gone far, however, when he no longer felt like whistling. He couldn't say why, but he just wasn't in the mood anymore. Then, as he walked farther, he began to feel edgy. The scenery looked different. The leaves on the trees looked leafy in a different way.

Now when Ordinary thought about his Dream, *it* looked different, too. For the first time, he saw how pursuing it could cause him a lot of discomfort. He would have to do unfamiliar things in unfamiliar places. And he wouldn't have his box to watch.

Then he had an even more disturbing thought: To do what he most loved, he would have to do what he most dreaded!

Ordinary's mood quickly went from edgy to anxious. His steps began to slow. And he began to have big doubts about his Big Dream. What had he been thinking? He *didn't* have enough talent or skill to succeed at his Dream. He was clearly Unable to accomplish Great Things. What if he failed right in front of other Nobodies?

Worse, even if he *could* do the Dream, he was clearly Unworthy. Any Nobody could see he didn't deserve to live his Dream. He was just Ordinary, after all. Maybe the Dream Giver had meant to give the Dream to some other Nobody more noble than him?

By now, each step was harder to take than the last. His anxiety grew into fear. Then up ahead he saw a sign. It read:

Leaving the Comfort Zone of Familiar.
Entering BorderLand.

Now Ordinary felt sheer terror. Sweat poured off his forehead. He could hardly breathe. He could hardly think.

Then, just as he came to the sign, Ordinary hit an invisible Wall of Fear.

He stopped, unable to take one more step.

He dropped his suitcase and sat on it.

∽

Should he turn around? he wondered. Or should he try to find a way to go on?

Time passed.

Then he heard these words: *Why are you stopping?*

Ordinary recognized the Dream Giver. "I think I want to go back home," he said weakly. "I'm not the right Nobody to go after such a Big Dream."

Yes, you are, said the Dream Giver. *I made you to do this.*

"But I don't think I *can* do this," he said.

Yes, you can. And I will be with you. I will help you.

✑

Ordinary stayed where he was. He watched an unfamiliar bug crawl across the toe of his shoe. Strange birds flew by overhead.

After a while, he stood and looked longingly toward the Unknown. Somewhere out there was his Big Dream.

But getting from here to there seemed way too hard.

Then he looked longingly back toward Familiar. He fondly remembered all its comforts—his Usual Job, his Best Friend, his recliner, his box. There *was* something wonderful about nothing happening.

Ordinary picked up his suitcase and decided to take one step in that direction, just to see what it felt like.

It felt better. Right away, his breathing came easier.

So he took another step—just to see what that step would feel like.

It felt even better.

He went on. With every step back toward the middle of Familiar, Ordinary grew more comfortable. But he quickly noticed he was also growing sad again. And he knew why: With each step he took, he was leaving his Big Dream farther behind.

Then he heard the Dream Giver again.

Why are you going back? he asked.

Ordinary stopped. "Because I'm afraid! Leaving Familiar feels too scary and too risky," he said.

Yes, it does.

"But if I was *supposed* to do this Big Dream," he

exclaimed, "then I'm sure I wouldn't feel so afraid!"

Yes, you would, said the Dream Giver. *Every Nobody does.*

Ordinary hung his head. He thought for a moment. "But *you* could take away the fear. *Please* take the fear away!" he begged. "If you don't, I can't go on!"

Yes, you can, the Dream Giver said. *Take courage, Ordinary.* And then he was gone.

❧

Ordinary saw his choice clearly now. He could either keep his comfort or his Dream.

But how do you "take courage" when you don't have any?

Ordinary decided. If his fear wasn't going to leave, he would have to go forward in spite of it.

Still trembling, he picked up his suitcase, turned his back on Familiar, and walked to the sign. And even though his fear kept growing, Ordinary shut his eyes and took a big step forward—right through the invisible Wall of Fear.

And there he made a surprising discovery.

On the other side of that single step—the exact one Ordinary didn't think he could take—he found that he had broken through his Comfort Zone.

Now the Wall of Fear was behind him. He was free, and his Dream was ahead.

He began to whistle again as he walked on, his Big Dream beating brightly in his chest.

Later that day...

Ordinary took out his journal and his long white feather and wrote down the Truth about his Comfort Zone.

- *It was hard to leave my Comfort Zone. But it would have been even harder to leave behind my Dream, and I'm glad I didn't.*

- *I still don't feel worthy or able to do my Dream, but the Dream Giver has promised to help me.*

- *Now I know a secret: I can "take courage," even when I feel afraid.*

- *My Big Dream was on the other side of that invisible Wall of Fear. I had to step through it. I didn't think I could, but I did.*

CHAPTER THREE

ORDINARY MEETS BULLIES IN THE BORDERLAND

*N*ot far past the sign, Ordinary's path sloped downward. Ahead he saw the Wide Waters and the bridge to the Unknown. Between him and the bridge lay the BorderLand, an open stretch of flat ground.

Ordinary was surprised to see, standing in the middle of the BorderLand, a few Nobodies from Familiar. One of the Nobodies, who looked more familiar than most, was hurrying toward him.

It was his Mother.

She rushed up and threw her arms around Ordinary. "Oh, Ordie!" she cried. "My baby! Thank goodness we got here in time!"

"But how did you get here so fast?" he asked.

"When you're not *really* leaving Familiar," she said, "you don't have to break through all that dreadful discomfort!"

"But why are you here?"

"You mustn't go on!" she said. "I was *so* alarmed when I heard you were leaving Familiar! I know you told us that you were, but I never thought you would. Honestly, what are you *thinking*? It's not safe! You could get hurt. You could even die!"

"But it's my Big Dream, Mother!" said Ordinary. "It's a wonderful Dream and I want to pursue it."

He tried to reassure his Mother. He told her that as Big Dreams go, his was only a little life threatening. But this seemed to alarm his Mother more than ever.

As they walked across the BorderLand, Ordinary spotted his Uncle and Best Friend.

Ordinary's Uncle strode up first. "So, you've decided to become a Dreamer," he said accusingly. "Do you realize that you are going completely against every tradition in this family? Why should *you* become a Somebody when the rest of us have always been happy being Nobodies?"

Before Ordinary could reply, Best Friend stepped in. "I was worried before, Ordinary," he said gravely, "but the more I've thought about it, the more convinced I am that you can't succeed at this. I can't stand by and watch you go down in defeat!"

Ordinary was speechless and bewildered. He'd heard a rumor about Border Bullies. But he had supposed that if it were true, Bullies would be Nobodies he didn't know. He never imagined they'd be some of the Nobodies who knew him best!

Now his Mother, Uncle, and Best Friend *all* stood silently before him, blocking his view of the bridge to his Big Dream. How would he ever get past them? Should he even try? He needed time to think.

He asked his Bullies to wait for him. Then he walked alone down to the water's edge, where he sat on a large rock.

Looking out over the Wide Waters, Ordinary thought and thought. He thought until he began to think that maybe his Bullies were right. Maybe he was wrong to pursue his Dream.

Then Ordinary heard a voice call his name. When he turned to see who it was, he recognized a Somebody. It was Champion, an old friend from Familiar who used to be a Nobody.

"Champion!" exclaimed Ordinary. "What are you doing here?"

Champion sat down on the rock beside him. "When I heard you had become a Dreamer, I just *had* to come," he said. "I knew you'd need help."

"Thanks," said Ordinary with a heavy sigh. "But did you see all my Bullies?"

"I saw them," said Champion. "They're Bullies, all right. But think of me as your Border Buster. I want to help you break through their opposition."

Then Champion helped Ordinary understand what was happening. "Your Mother, Uncle, and Best Friend are only doing what's natural," he said. "When you left your Comfort Zone, you really shook up theirs. Each of them has something to lose if you go forward."

"That makes sense," said Ordinary. "But what do I do now? How do I get all my Bullies on my side?"

"Well, you might not be able to. Wisdom is the key. Try to understand what's motivating them. Look for the merit of their concerns. Some Bullies you need to simply dismiss or avoid. But most Border Bullies have concerns that can help you clarify your plans. That's how a Dreamer turns opposition into opportunity."

When Champion stood to leave, he said, "Hold fast to your Dream, Ordinary. You're going to be a Somebody someday. I just know it!"

Then he shook Ordinary's hand and jumped down from the rock. "Remember," he said, "when Bullies try to block your way, what matters most is who you choose to please!"

Ordinary thought about Champion's parting words. He decided it was time to talk to his Bullies again.

As the sun began to set, he walked back and forth along the water's edge, talking with them. He told them more about his Dream. He learned from their concerns.

Then he told them he had decided to pursue his Dream into the Unknown.

By sundown, Ordinary was ready to cross the Border. As Mother handed him his suitcase, he saw tears in her eyes.

"I've changed my mind. I want you to pursue your Dream," she said. "And your Father will be so proud of you. I think he wishes he had taken the same journey years ago." Then she hugged him good-bye.

Ordinary shook hands with Best Friend and his Uncle (who still did not look pleased). While the three watched, he walked toward the bridge over the Wide Waters.

In the gathering dusk, Ordinary had failed to notice that another Nobody stood on the Bridge. But this Nobody was not just any Nobody—he was the Landlord of Familiar. He was the one who decided what was right for Nobodies. He owned every inch of the land. He even owned the bridge.

"I am denying you access to my bridge," he said.

"But why?" asked Ordinary.

"Because I need every Nobody to stay in Familiar at their Usual Job," said the Landlord. "I won't lose any more Nobodies to this silly notion of Dreams. I will not let you go!"

Ordinary tried hard not to panic. Wisdom told him that an antagonist like the Landlord was the worst kind of Bully. He had a lot to lose *and* he didn't care about Ordinary.

What should he do now? What *could* he do? Then
Ordinary remembered Champion's parting words.

And that's when he decided to swim.

He knew he might not make it. The Wide Waters
were very wide, and he wasn't a very strong swimmer. But
he had to try.

While his Bullies looked on, Ordinary walked down to
the Wide Waters. He was about to step in when something
caught his eye. A small boat was moored nearby.

When he got closer, Ordinary saw a note on the seat
of the boat. He picked it up and read:

> *Ordinary, if you've found this boat, I know you've chosen to*
> *please the Dream Giver. Enjoy a dry crossing! Your Dream is*
> *waiting for you in the Land of Promise. I promise!*
> *— Champion*

Ordinary untied the boat, stowed his suitcase in the
front of the boat, and shoved off.

As he rowed out into the Wide Waters, Ordinary
watched his Border Bullies grow smaller and smaller.
When he was sure that he had finally, really left Familiar,
he waved his last good-byes to the Nobodies on the shore.

But by then it was too dark to tell if they waved back.

That very night...

Before he went to sleep in the tall, dry grass on the other side of the Waters, Ordinary used the feather again to write in his journal.

- I met Bullies at the BorderLand— they were Nobodies I knew!

- When I left Familiar, it upset the Comfort Zone of those close to me. They felt like they were losing something important.

- Even though my Bullies tried to stop me, some of their concerns will help me.

- I couldn't sway all my Bullies. In the end, I had to decide who I would please. I chose to please the Dream Giver.

CHAPTER FOUR

ORDINARY ENTERS
THE WASTELAND

*O*rdinary slept deeply and woke humming his unfamiliar tune. The fears of leaving his Comfort Zone were gone now. His Border Bullies were behind him.

His step was light as he traveled into the Unknown. Around each new bend, he expected to reach the Land of Promise where he would find his Big Dream.

But he didn't find it. Instead, he soon found himself at the edge of a wide chasm. A haze obscured the view below. When he reached the bottom, he saw what lay ahead. And what he saw made his heart sink. He saw miles and miles of nothing but sand, rocks, and a few scraggly trees.

He was standing on the edge of an empty WasteLand.

How could any wonderful Dream live here? he thought.

He wasn't sure. But the path continued on, curving away into the dreary distance. So he decided to go on.

∾

Ordinary walked. And walked. Every time he got hungry, he opened his suitcase and ate. And every time he got thirsty, he opened it and drank. And every time he thought about his Dream, he decided to keep going.

Time passed. Ordinary's skin burned. His feet blistered. His bones ached. One day blurred into another. And then one day he got hungry and opened his case...and *didn't* find anything to eat.

That was the day Ordinary began to worry. He called out to the Dream Giver for food. But he got no answer.

Two days later, he ran out of water. He called out to the Dream Giver again. And again, he heard nothing.

Fortunately, that was also the day Ordinary managed to find a trickle of water coming from a rock. At least now he was only starving. But if he was smart enough to find water, maybe he could find food, too.

Sure enough, it wasn't too long before he spotted a strange bush with some strange desert fruit hanging from its branches. Ordinary tried one. It didn't taste sweet, but it didn't taste sour, either. So he ate his fill.

Still, the Dream Giver was nowhere in sight.

∾

More time passed. The longest hours and days Ordinary could ever remember passed. Desperately, he began to look for a way out.

One day he followed what looked like a shortcut over a ridge. But it led to a canyon that ended in quicksand.

He tried traveling at night when it was cooler. But he kept losing the trail.

Every delay made him more determined to find a quicker route. But every attempt only led to another dead end.

Again and again, Ordinary lost his way. Again and again, he cried out for the Dream Giver to show him the way. But no answer came. Why had he ever trusted the Dream Giver to guide him in the first place?

The day came when Ordinary finally gave up. He sat on his suitcase and refused to move until the Dream Giver showed up with a plan.

But the Dream Giver didn't show up that day. Or the next.

Ordinary had never felt so lost and alone. He became angry. He got angrier and angrier.

And then a hard, hot wind began to blow.

The wind blew all that day and all the next. Sand blew into Ordinary's eyes. It blew into his teeth and ears.

When the wind finally stopped, Ordinary stood to his feet. But as far as he could see, there was only sand. The path to his Dream had disappeared completely. Obviously, his entire trip through the WasteLand had been a Waste!

Hot tears coursed down his dirty cheeks. "You're not a Dream Giver," he shouted at the sky. "You're a Dream

Taker! I trusted you. You promised to be with me and help me. And you didn't!"

Then Ordinary stumbled in despair across the sandy Waste, dragging his empty suitcase behind him. His Dream was dead, and now he wanted to die, too.

When he came to a scraggly tree, he lay down in its scraggly patch of shade and closed his eyes.

That night, he slept the sleep of a dreamless Dreamer.

∽

The next morning, Ordinary heard something. Startled, he peered up to see a shimmering Somebody sitting in the branches of the tree.

"Who are you?" he asked, as she climbed down to the ground.

"My name is Faith," she said. "The Dream Giver sent me to help you."

"But it's too late!" cried Ordinary. "My Dream is dead. When I needed the Dream Giver most, he was nowhere in sight."

"What do you need that you haven't received?" asked Faith.

"Well, if it weren't for the few springs of water I found," answered Ordinary, "I'd be dead of thirst by now!"

"Yes? And?" she asked.

"If it weren't for the fruit I found, I'd be a walking skeleton!" he replied. "Wait! I *am* a walking skeleton! I could die of starvation any minute!"

"Oh, my!" Faith murmured. "And?"

"Well," huffed Ordinary, "a little guidance would have been nice. Ever since I came here, it's been one delay after another. I've been wandering in circles since I don't know when. What a Waste!"

"I see," said Faith, nodding. "So what will you do now?"

"Just tell me how to get back to Familiar," he said.

"I'm sorry," she said. "But I can't help you with that."

"That figures," said Ordinary. "The Dream Giver sends me a helper who can't even help!"

"You might be right," said Faith. "But that's for you to decide."

Then Faith walked away in a direction Ordinary felt sure was wrong.

❧

It wasn't long before Ordinary began to have second thoughts. What if *he* was wrong? He wished he hadn't been so rude to the Somebody named Faith. And he began to miss her. He realized that while they were talking, he had felt hope for the first time in a very long time.

Ordinary jumped to his feet and scanned the horizon.

"Faith!" he cried. But she was nowhere in sight.

"Faith!" he cried again. But there was no reply.

Then Ordinary had an idea. He climbed the scraggly tree to the top. From there, he could see Faith in the distance. As quickly as he could, he climbed down and set off in the same direction.

Later that same day, Ordinary was eating some fruit beside a trickle of water, when he saw his journey through the WasteLand in a whole new way.

Food enough for the day.

Water, when he needed to drink.

A path to follow that led to Faith.

How could he have been so blind? Even when the Dream Giver had been nowhere in sight, he had always been near.

That was the day, too, that Ordinary looked at his empty suitcase and decided it was time to leave it behind.

He made a makeshift knapsack, took his Dream Journal and feather and ink, and walked on.

After that, whenever Ordinary came to a scraggly tree, he climbed it to look for Faith. And when he had her in sight, he marked the direction and started walking again.

One day, Ordinary met some Dreamers returning to Familiar. They told him a sad story. They had crossed the WasteLand and nearly reached the Land of Promise. But then they encountered Giants so large and overwhelming that the Dreamers felt as small as grasshoppers. And the Dream Giver had been nowhere in sight.

The Nobodies sounded convincing. And he recognized their weariness. But as they continued talking, he saw something more: They had stopped trusting the

Dream Giver, and now they were traveling in the opposite direction from Faith.

When the Nobodies strongly warned him that what lay ahead was too hard, he saw something else. *He* had changed. His trip through the WasteLand had not been a Waste. Now he was prepared for what lay ahead, no matter how hard.

"Travel safely," he told the returning Nobodies. "But I'll be going on."

As Ordinary pressed on through the desert, his Dream beat brightly in his chest again. And the more the sun blazed, the more Ordinary believed that he could find the Land of Promise, no matter how long it took—if only he took the way of Faith.

One morning on the far side of the desert...

Ordinary wrote down the Truth about the WasteLand.

- After crossing the Waters, I thought my Dream was just around the corner. Instead, I found a WasteLand.

- I was disappointed by the delay. And my doubts about the Dream Giver only made things worse.

- Now I see that the WasteLand was not a Waste! It has taught me to trust the Dream Giver, even when he's nowhere in sight.

- I think I am stronger now. I'm following faith, and every day I feel more prepared for whatever lies ahead.

CHAPTER FIVE

ORDINARY FINDS SANCTUARY

*O*ne night, Ordinary dreamed that the Dream Giver was standing near him. *Well done, Ordinary!* the Dream Giver said. *Come to my Sanctuary.*

When Ordinary awoke, he was beside a gurgling stream. How he had arrived there, or when, he wasn't sure. But the WasteLand was behind him.

He wondered at his dream and hoped it was true. Was the Dream Giver pleased with him? Was Sanctuary a real place, and could it be nearby?

He picked up his knapsack and decided to follow the stream into the lush mountain forest he saw ahead. Something seemed to be drawing him onward and upward, he couldn't say what. But it felt like an Invitation.

❦

Before long, giant trees towered over Ordinary. Walking across the floor of the forest, he felt hushed and small and swallowed up by Greatness.

Then he began to climb. Higher and higher he climbed, following the stream, until suddenly he entered a level clearing filled with bright light.

His heart told him that this was Sanctuary, and he was in the presence of the Dream Giver.

Come to the water, he heard the Dream Giver say.

Ahead of him in the clearing he saw a small waterfall that fed a pool of still waters. He walked to the edge, then slipped into the purest water he had ever seen. He floated and splashed, sending diamonds of light spraying through the air.

Time passed. But it didn't seem to pass at all.

When Ordinary emerged from the pool, the last traces of the WasteLand had been washed away.

❦

Ordinary stayed in the clearing filled with light for many days. The Dream Giver had never felt so close—as present now as he had felt absent in the WasteLand.

Then Ordinary heard the Dream Giver's voice again. *Come into the light.*

That's when Ordinary noticed that the light, which

had been shining all around him, was now shining *through* him.

Trembling, he looked. And he saw into his heart. He saw things he had said and done that he did not want to see. He saw rebellion and selfishness and betrayal. And everywhere he looked, he saw darkness.

Tears began streaming down his cheeks. "Take away my darkness," he pleaded. "Give me your light!"

And the Dream Giver did. He took away Ordinary's darkness and gave him his light.

Then the Dream Giver said, *Come closer to me.*

And Ordinary did.

Again and again, Ordinary came deeper into the light. And the further he came, the more he felt at one with the Dream Giver.

Then the Dream Giver spoke again.

Come higher, he said.

❧

Ordinary started up the mountain again, his step light. He couldn't wait to discover what the Dream Giver had in store for him.

Before long, Ordinary emerged at a summit. He found himself standing on a broad table of rock, gazing out at a glorious sight—a river below, then a wide valley, and above it, all along the far horizon, a gleaming ribbon of shining hills.

"The Land of Promise!" Ordinary gasped. "It has to be!"

Yes, he heard the Dream Giver say.

Ordinary let out a shout of victory. "I made it! My Big Dream is right over there!" he yelled.

Yes.

Ordinary was overcome with happiness. His Big Dream was finally within reach. Oh, how he wished that Best Friend and his Parents and every Nobody in Familiar could be here to see what he was seeing at this moment!

Ordinary, said the Dream Giver.

"Yes," said Ordinary.

Give me your Dream.

"What do you mean?" Ordinary asked. "It's my Dream. You're the one who gave it to me."

Yes. And now I'm asking you to give it back.

Ordinary was shocked, but he didn't even have to think. "I can't," he told the Dream Giver. "And I won't."

Ordinary paced back and forth along the rim of the summit, trying to understand what had just happened. Why would the Dream Giver want to take away his Big Dream? How could he even ask? Especially now, when Ordinary had come so far.

It wasn't fair. It wasn't even right.

Then Ordinary had an idea. Maybe there was a way out. "Do I *have* to give it back?" he asked.

No, the Dream Giver said. *Some choose not to.*

So he had a choice. He *could* keep his Dream. But instead of relief at the thought, Ordinary felt confused and sad. What was he going to do?

He slumped down on the rock. He thought for a long while. Finally, he saw what was at stake.

He could please the Dream Giver and surrender his Dream. Or he could go against the Dream Giver's wishes and keep his Dream, but risk losing the Dream Giver's pleasure.

The choice broke his heart.

Time passed. Ordinary thought, and thought some more. The sun set and rose again.

In the morning light, his eyes fell on a smooth, flat stone nearby. Picking it up, he noticed that the stone fit perfectly in his palm. Then he saw a word etched into its surface.

Remember.

What could it mean? he wondered. Was the stone a message from the Dream Giver or from another Dreamer? What should he remember?

Holding the stone, Ordinary found himself thinking back. He remembered Champion and Faith. They must have faced this choice. What would they say to him now?

He remembered the returning Dreamers. He could still hear their sad and bitter voices. They couldn't have surrendered their Dreams here—they didn't even trust the Dream Giver!

Over and over he turned the stone in his palm. Finally, his thoughts turned to the Dream Giver. The

Dream Giver had always kept his promises. He had always been good to Ordinary, even when he was nowhere in sight and nothing seemed to make sense.

Then Ordinary knew what he had to do—no, what he *wanted* to do.

He carried his knapsack to the edge of the rock and sat down. He took out his journal and his long white feather, and he wrote his last entry about his Big Dream.

> *I am surrendering my Dream to you, Dream Giver. I've decided that it's you that I can't go on without.*

Then Ordinary left his journal open on the rock. He wouldn't be needing it any longer. He put the feather and stone in his bag and began his slow descent to the river below.

∽

Later that day, Ordinary reached the river. No one waited for him there. He had no Dream or plan now. Yet he felt a deep peace.

He waded into the river and swam across, pulling his knapsack behind him. At the far bank, he climbed out. And the first thing he saw was his journal, lying open on the grass.

His heart racing, he picked it up and read:

Ordinary, I am giving you back your Dream. Now you can use it to serve me. Now you can achieve truly Great Things. And I am with you always.

Ordinary knelt by the riverbank and wept with joy. The Dream Giver was more kind, more good, more wonderful and trustworthy than he had ever imagined.

Now when Ordinary looked at his surrendered Dream, he saw that it had grown. Now his Dream was no longer only about Ordinary. Now it was part of the Dream Giver's Big Dream for the whole world.

When Ordinary stood to leave, he noticed on the rise above the river a memorial built of stones. Every stone was smooth and small and had the word *Remember* etched on its surface. Standing by the monument to the Dream Giver's goodness, Ordinary felt awed, and surrounded by many witnesses.

Carefully, he placed his own stone at the top of the memorial.

And he walked on.

That evening by the light of the moon...

Ordinary pulled his journal out of his knapsack and wrote about his time in Sanctuary.

- I will never be the same after Sanctuary. I swam in still waters there and washed away the last traces of the WasteLand.

- The Dream Giver's light revealed the darkness inside me. It was unbearable. How could he want me to come any closer? But he took away my darkness.

- When the Dream Giver asked me to give my Dream to him, I didn't think I could. But I wanted the Dream Giver more than my Dream, so I did.

- The Dream Giver gave my Dream back to me. Now it is part of his Big Dream—and that means my Dream is a lot bigger than before. May I always use it to serve him!

CHAPTER SIX

ORDINARY REACHES THE VALLEY OF GIANTS

*I*n the morning, Ordinary entered a broad valley that seemed to lead up to the Land of Promise. But soon he came upon a sign that read:

Beware, Dreamer!
Valley of the Giants

Ordinary stared at the sign. So the returning Dreamers were right. Giants were real.

What should he do? He had no weapons. He had no plan. But his Big Dream was bigger than ever. And he trusted the Dream Giver.

So he decided to press on.

᠃

Ordinary hadn't gone far when he heard giant footsteps. He hurried to hide behind a bush. He was *not* yet ready to face a Giant!

But when Ordinary peered around a leaf, he didn't see a Giant obstacle, but a mighty Being.

"Hail, brave Warrior!" the Being called out.

"Who, me?" Ordinary asked in a small voice.

"Yes. You, behind that bush."

"I'm no Warrior," mumbled Ordinary, stepping out from behind the bush. He'd never felt so foolish. "I'm a Nobody from the Land of Familiar," he said.

"Every Nobody who comes this far is a Warrior," said the Being. "I'm the Commander. The Dream Giver sent me to help you defeat your Giants."

"He did? I *do* need help!" said Ordinary eagerly. "Compared to a Giant, I'm small and weak."

"Don't be afraid of any Giant, Ordinary," said the Commander. "They're real. They're enormous. They block the path to your Dream. But if you believe in the Dream Giver and you're willing to take a Big Risk, you will get past them."

"But I have no weapons or armor!" exclaimed Ordinary.

Then the Commander helped Ordinary see how the Dream Giver had been preparing him for battle since the day he left Familiar. "All the Truths you've learned on your journey so far will serve as your weapons and armor," he said.

"But how will I know what to do?" asked Ordinary.

"The Dream Giver will tell you, and he will give you his power if you ask for it."

Ordinary felt reassured. But he still didn't feel like a Warrior.

"Beware of Unbelief, Ordinary," said the Commander. "Unbelief is much more dangerous to your Dream than any Giant!"

And then the Commander was gone.

Ordinary hadn't gone far up the Valley when he met his first Giant. It was enormous, all right! And it completely blocked the path to his Dream.

When it noticed Ordinary, the Giant yawned in his direction. "Where do you think you're going, little Nobody?"

Ordinary recognized the Giant towering over him. It was Moneyless.

"I need to get past," said Ordinary.

"Sure you do. Everybody does," the Giant said.

Ordinary tried to think of a plan, but none came to mind. "So...I need you to get out of my way," he said.

"I'm not moving," said the Giant. "I guess you'll have to move me yourself."

For a moment, Ordinary hesitated. Then he cried out, "Dream Giver, help me! Please give me your power!"

And the Dream Giver did. Then he told Ordinary what to do and what to say.

Ordinary looked up at the Giant called Moneyless and shouted, "I challenge you in the name of the Dream Giver!" Then he attacked the Giant with all his weapons and armor.

At first the Giant didn't move. But Ordinary kept reaching for the Truths he had learned. He took courage. He believed that the Dream Giver would provide. He relied on Wisdom. He fought on. He endured.

And with every advance, he felt the Dream Giver's pleasure.

Finally, the day came when Moneyless did retreat. Ordinary's cry of victory rang through the Valley. "Great and good is the Dream Giver!" he cried.

After that victory, Ordinary never doubted again that he was a Warrior.

As Ordinary traveled up the Valley, he met more Giants. Some, like Moneyless, were obstacles that he had to get around. Some, like Corruption, opposed his Dream and fought him fiercely. Some, like Rejection, attacked him personally and left him deeply wounded.

But Ordinary met other Dreamers, too. During seasons of rest, they gathered to tell stories about the Dream Giver and encourage each other.

From other Dreamers, Ordinary learned to see a bigger picture: Every Giant was another opportunity for the Dream Giver to receive honor.

Higher and higher, Ordinary moved up the Valley, battling Giants on the way to his Dream. One day, Ordinary came across a Wounded Warrior lying on a quiet hill.

Ordinary dropped down by her side. "How can I help you?" he asked.

"My wounds are too many and great," she said. "This will be my dying place."

⌒

Ordinary's heart broke. "But why would the Dream Giver let you be defeated?" Ordinary asked. "You've come so far. You have to finish your Big Dream!"

She had no reply.

Night fell. The Wounded Warrior grew weaker. Finally, in the darkness, she said, "Tell me the Name of your Dream."

After Ordinary did, the Warrior was quiet for a time. Then she spoke. "That is the Name of my Dream, also," she said. "I fought Giants ahead of you. You will fight more after me. But we have the same Big Dream."

In the first light of dawn, she spoke for the last time. "Death is not my defeat," she whispered. "It is my victory."

That morning, Ordinary buried his Warrior friend on the hilltop. Then he sat for a long time, looking across the hills and valleys. He thought about the Warrior's life, and about her death. He thought about her dying words.

And he became certain that he would not have gotten

this far on the path to his Dream if his friend had not gone before him.

Finally, Ordinary took his long white feather and wrote the Truth on her headstone:

Here lies a Mighty Warrior.
She finished her Dream.

᠆᠆

Soon after leaving the hill, Ordinary began to sense that he was almost through the Valley of Giants. He was getting closer to the place where he could do what he wanted to do most. And he walked faster in anticipation.

Then one day, just as he caught a glimpse of the high country ahead, he stumbled upon a small camp of ragged Anybodies. Ordinary had never met any Anybodies, but he'd heard of them. They were a lot like Nobodies.

The Anybodies told him they were from the City of Anybodies that lay just ahead. A Giant of Darkness oppressed the city from his stronghold at the gates. No Anybody could leave or enter. It had been that way for so long that no Anybody could remember how long it had been that way.

When Ordinary asked about the Dream Giver, the Anybodies just shook their heads. Few believed in him. Other Warriors had mentioned his name, they said, but they had passed by without challenging their Giant.

Should he pass by, too? He couldn't wait to find his
Big Dream.

Then Ordinary heard the Dream Giver's voice. He
said, *Prepare for battle.*

❦

Word spread quickly through the camp. The Warrior
named Ordinary was about to challenge the Giant of
Darkness in the name of the Dream Giver.

Anybodies crowded around the Giant's stronghold to
watch.

Ordinary walked up to the gate and cried, "Giant of
Darkness, in the name of the Dream Giver, I come to
defeat you! I proclaim deliverance for every Anybody in
the camp and every Anybody in the city!"

When the Giant burst out of its stronghold, the
Anybodies gasped. "None of these Anybodies will ever be
free!" the Giant roared. "Their lives are worthless! Their
hopes are lies!" Then he attacked with the heaviest chains
of darkness that Ordinary had ever seen.

Ordinary fought courageously. He fought with the
Dream Giver's power, and he used every weapon and
piece of armor he had. All day, the sound of warfare
crashed through the Valley.

But by midafternoon, any Anybody could see that
Ordinary was growing weaker while the Giant was as
strong as ever.

Ordinary retreated to the edge of the field and cried
out to the Dream Giver, "Are you with me?"

Yes, the Dream Giver said.

"This Giant is too strong for me," gasped Ordinary.

Yes, it is.

"A victory will take a miracle!" said Ordinary.

Yes, it will.

"So what should I do?"

Prepare for a miracle, said the Dream Giver. *Lay down your weapons. Take only your feather. And you will bring me Great Honor.*

Leave his weapons?

Unbelief swept through Ordinary's heart. What the Dream Giver asked was impossible!

Then Ordinary remembered. He remembered surrendering his Dream, and getting it back even bigger and better than before. He remembered the Dream Giver's goodness in the WasteLand, even when he was nowhere in sight. He remembered the Dying Warrior's victory. And he remembered his Big Dream...

And that's when Ordinary turned away from Unbelief and decided to take a Big Risk for the Dream Giver.

He put down his weapons.

Every Anybody groaned in disappointment.

Then Ordinary picked up his knapsack and pulled out his feather and walked toward the Giant.

The Anybodies gasped in disbelief.

But the Giant only laughed. "Are you going to knock me over with a feather?" it roared.

Ordinary wasn't sure what to do or say until the Giant of Darkness towered over him. Then the Dream Giver told him just what to do.

He raised his long white feather high above his head, and as he did, it grew heavy in his hand, as heavy as a sword.

"If the Dream Giver is for me," Ordinary shouted, "what Giant can stand against me?"

Then he swung the feather in a mighty arc, right across the Giant's evil heart. And when he swung, an amazing thing happened.

Chains scattered in pieces. Darkness fled. And the Giant collapsed in a heap, defeated, at Ordinary's feet.

The Anybodies knew a miracle when they saw one.

Soon a noisy, happy procession led Ordinary past the defeated Giant, around his dark stronghold, and up to the gates of their city. With every step, the joyful Anybodies sang praises. But the praises were not for Ordinary.

"The Dream Giver is good!" they sang. "The Dream Giver is strong! Victory belongs to the Dream Giver!"

For the first time that any Anybody could remember, they were free.

Sitting by the Warrior's grave...

Ordinary took his feather and wrote the Truth about the Valley of Giants.

- I met a friend who shared my Dream and helped make it happen.

- Before I met my first Giant, I met the Commander. He told me that I am a Warrior! He showed me that my weapons are every Truth I've learned on my journey.

- Unbelief is dangerous. So far, I have chosen to Believe. But it feels risky every time.

- Even though I've been prepared to face my Giants, I still need the Dream Giver's power. Every time I defeat a Giant, the Dream Giver receives honor. Giants beware!

CHAPTER SEVEN

ORDINARY THRIVES IN THE LAND OF PROMISE

When Ordinary passed through the Anybodies' city gates, he saw hope and joy on every face. "Thank you, Warrior!" the Anybodies shouted. "Thank you for helping us!"

But the celebration hadn't moved far into the city when Ordinary began to see signs of want and need. He was shocked to see that some Anybodies lived in the dirt. Some lived in homes built out of sticks and mud.

Still, all day and all night, the celebration filled the streets of the city.

The next day, grateful Anybodies begged Ordinary to stay with them for a while.

"Yes," he said, "but only for a short time." He still had a Big Dream to pursue. He could picture the city where he would accomplish his Dream more clearly now than ever. It was a beautiful city with white marble walls, and it shone with promise in his heart.

And it felt very, very near.

❧

In the days that followed, Ordinary walked through every street and lane and path of the dismal City of Anybodies. He talked to young Anybodies and old Anybodies. And what he saw and heard filled him with sadness.

Yes, the Giant of Darkness was gone. But years of tyranny had left the city damaged and broken. The needs of the Anybodies were great, and their hopes were few.

Ordinary's heart began to ache in a way it had never ached before.

❧

One day, Ordinary took a stroll near the city gates. As he walked, he talked with the friendly Anybody children who followed him.

Then he heard the Dream Giver say, *What do you see?*

Ordinary stopped. He looked down into the children's faces. "I see beautiful Anybodies in great need," he said.

Yes, said the Dream Giver. *What else do you see?*

Then Ordinary looked up. He could hardly believe his eyes. Carved on the inside of the gate was the Name of his Dream!

Your Big Dream lies here, the Dream Giver said.

Could it be true?

Instantly, he knew it was true. He had arrived!

Then Ordinary understood why he hadn't recognized his Big Dream when it was right in front of him. The lovely city he'd imagined all along was not his Dream— but a picture of what his Dream would accomplish.

The Big Needs of these Anybodies matched perfectly the Big Dream in his heart. And it was time to *do* his Dream.

Ordinary was so excited that he let go with a whoop of joy, much to the delight of the Anybody children.

The next morning, Ordinary woke up early, ready to begin. Of course, he had no idea where to begin. There were so many needs that he was overwhelmed. He was just one Dreamer.

But he decided to begin at the beginning. He saw the need nearest him and tried to meet it. He spent what he had. He did what he could. He used what he knew. Every day, he asked the Dream Giver to help and guide him.

And things began to change for the Anybodies.

Time passed, and Ordinary worked hard. Doing his Dream could be difficult, but Ordinary had never felt more fulfilled. He was building something new from something broken. He was meeting Big Needs while doing what he loved to do most.

One day, two more Dreamers arrived in the city. For many days, they walked the streets and talked to Anybodies, young and old. Then they told Ordinary that the City of Anybodies was the city of their Dreams, too.

Immediately, Ordinary saw that it was true. The two Dreamers had resources that Ordinary lacked. They had skills he had never learned. They could meet important Big Needs that Ordinary couldn't!

That was a very good day for Ordinary, and for the Anybodies, too.

∾

More time passed. Ordinary's devotion to the Dream Giver grew. He always did what the Dream Giver told him to do. He was careful to remember what the Dream Giver had done. And he worked hard to protect his Dream from compromise.

Then one day, Ordinary made a surprising discovery.

An Anybody had told Ordinary that he didn't enjoy his work very much. And Ordinary had noticed that he wasn't very good at it, either.

Ordinary asked him, "What do you love to do most?"

When he answered, Ordinary saw the problem. There wasn't much opportunity here for this Anybody to do what he loved. Ordinary thought for a moment.

"Do Anybodies have Big Dreams?" he asked.

"I wish," the Anybody said wistfully. "I wish I had a Big Dream."

"But it seems like you do!" exclaimed Ordinary. He thought some more. Then he asked, "Have you always lived here?"

"Yes," he said.

"So this is familiar to you, right?"

"Yes," he said. "It's *very* familiar. I'm comfortable here. I find the routines reliable. But sometimes it feels like something big is missing, or that I—"

"Say no more!" cried Ordinary.

That evening, Ordinary taught the village of Anybodies his unfamiliar tune. Only now that he was a Somebody living his Dream, he knew the words, too.

It was a song about the special place that every Anybody has in the Dream Giver's heart.

It was a song about how every Anybody is made to be Somebody Special and accomplish Great Things.

After that, a lot of Anybodies began waking up to their Big Dream. Some found that the city of their Dream was the City of Anybodies. Others set off on journeys of their own.

And not long after that, the City began to look a lot like the picture of the Big Dream that Ordinary had carried in his heart for so long. More and more, the City's walls gleamed in the sun like white marble, and its streets shone with promise.

Then one day, Ordinary thought he heard the Dream Giver say, *Come further...*

Ordinary found himself walking, knapsack over his shoulder, along the far wall at the back of the city. He noticed a little gate he'd never noticed before.

He heard the Dream Giver again. *Come further.*

He opened the gate and stepped outside. But as he did, he felt strangely...uncomfortable. He looked toward the distant Unknown.

Well done, Ordinary! the Dream Giver said. *You are a good and faithful Dreamer. Now let me show you more.*

"More?" asked Ordinary.

More, said the Dream Giver. *There's so much more of my Big Dream waiting for you.*

Now Ordinary looked at the horizon again. And he saw many Valleys and Wide Waters. And he saw the gleam of many more Lands of Promise waiting for a Dreamer to claim for the Dream Giver.

Soon you will leave what is familiar once again, the Dream Giver said. *And I will be with you.*

Suddenly, Ordinary understood. His Big Dream in the City of Anybodies was nearly done. He was ready now for the Dream to grow into a new and bigger Dream.

Soon it would be time to pursue it.

Ordinary looked again toward what lay in his future. The horizon was *full* of promise.

"Thank you, Dream Giver!" Ordinary whispered. "Thank you for the gift of my Big Dream."

And he began to hum an unfamiliar tune.

Dear Father,

I'm writing to you after a very long journey... but I made it! I'm living in the Land of Promise and watching my Big Dream happen all around me. And to think it all started with sticks and mud when I was a boy!

Father, I discovered that every Nobody has a Dream, and it's never too late to pursue it! I know you thought your Dream died, but a Big Dream never dies. Your Dream is here somewhere, waiting for you. And if you don't pursue it, something very important won't happen.

Of course, Mother has a Big Dream, too! I can't wait to see both of you!

Father, as you see, I'm sending you my feather. It will help you on your journey. It will lead you straight toward a miracle that has your name on it.

I miss you!

Love, your son,

Ordinary

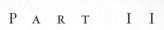

PART II

THE JOURNEY
TO YOUR
BIG DREAM

MEET YOUR
DREAM COACH

I hope you enjoyed the story of Ordinary and his journey to achieve his Big Dream. Most of us can relate to the character of Ordinary because at times we feel very ordinary ourselves. In a world as vast and impersonal as ours, it's easy to feel like a Nobody, isn't it?

But the truth Ordinary discovered from the Dream Giver is that every Nobody was made to be a Somebody. And the key to discovering all you are meant to do and be is to wake up to the Big Dream God has given you and set out on a journey to achieve it.

In the coming chapters, that's what I want to help you do. Think of me as your travel guide, or Dream Coach. My advice comes from years of experience as a Dreamer and incorporates the lessons others have taught me along the way. More important, the insights and principles I'll share are based on the timeless truths of the Bible.

Not surprisingly, the Bible story that most clearly shows these principles at work is the epic story of Israel's journey from Egypt to the Promised Land. We'll use that story, especially as it was lived out by Moses and Joshua, to uncover the secrets of successful Dreamers.

The story of the Exodus reveals a pattern that is repeated throughout the Bible whenever God's people reach for their Dream and attempt great things for Him. In almost every instance, they:

1. Become aware of a personal Dream or calling, then decide to pursue it.
2. Face fear as they leave a place of comfort.
3. Encounter opposition from those around them.
4. Endure a season of difficulty that tests their faith.
5. Learn the importance of surrender and consecration to God.
6. Fight the Giants that stand between them and the fulfillment of their Dream.
7. Reach their full potential as they achieve their Dream and bring honor to God.

The good news for every Dreamer is that each stage or obstacle along our journey is intended not to *block* our dream, but to help us *break through* to the fulfillment God promises.

Like Ordinary, I can count as many scars as successes on the journey to my Dream. The way of the Dreamer is difficult—but anything less is hardly living at all! In fact, I've discovered that it's the *only* way you and I can find true fulfillment and become all that God created us to be.

Isn't it time to begin? You've waited long enough.

Your dream is beating in your chest.

Do you feel it?

Tell your friends the news.

Pack your bags.

It's time to follow the Dream Giver on the journey to *your* Dream.

CHAPTER EIGHT

YOU WERE BORN
FOR THIS

One morning, Ordinary woke up with these words echoing in his mind: What you're missing, you already have...

Could it be? Ordinary looked and looked. And then he discovered that in a small corner of his heart lay a Big Dream. The Big Dream told him that he, a Nobody, was made to be a Somebody and destined to achieve Great Things.

The Hollywood producer didn't believe it was true, and I couldn't seem to change his mind, even though I was about to buy him lunch at my favorite neighborhood restaurant. He couldn't believe that every person has been created with a Big Dream, and that most people, for one reason or another, just aren't pursuing it.

He said only a few people are "born dreamers."

"Just because you happen to be one of them," he said, "you don't really think everyone in this restaurant is one, do you?"

I was losing the debate as we took our seats, and I
didn't know what to do. Our conversation had special
meaning to me because, although my producer friend didn't
know it, I was trying to help him pursue *his* Big Dream.

I was almost to the point of giving up when an idea
came to mind. Why not try to prove it right in front of
him?

When our waitress Sonja came to take our order, my
heart was pounding. But I took a risk. I asked her, "Are
you doing what you've always wished you could be
doing?"

She looked at me questioningly. "What do you mean?"
she asked.

I said, "Well, maybe you *are* doing your dream, and
that would be terrific. But I wonder, do you have a Big
Dream inside of your heart that hasn't come true yet?"

Sonja thought for a moment. Then she said, "My
mother is a nurse. My sister is a nurse. And I always
dreamed of becoming a nurse."

"Would you have been a good nurse?" I asked.

Sonja became emotional. "I would have been a really
good nurse," she said softly.

"Would you like to be a nurse at this very moment?" I
asked.

"Yes," she said.

So I took another risk. "Do you happen to believe
that God wants you to be a nurse?" I asked.

She looked away for a minute, then said, "I think so."

"If God wants you to be a nurse, then there must be a way for you to be one," I said. "What has stopped you?"

Sonja listed the reasons: an education cut short by marriage, then two children, then the demands of raising a family. "Now it's impossible," she said. "It's too late." I heard the sadness in her voice.

"What would have to happen for you to become a nurse?" I asked.

"We don't have enough money," she said. "I can't afford a babysitter, so I can't go to school."

"So if you had a babysitter, you would go to school?" I asked.

"Yes," she said without hesitation.

I glanced at my producer friend to make sure he was taking this all in. Then I took another risk. "Sonja, I believe there's somebody in your life who cares about you and would babysit your children for free. Who is that person?"

Sonja thought for a moment, then her face lit up. "It's my mother!" she exclaimed. "She just retired two months ago! She loves her grandchildren. And she's always wanted me to have my dream. She'd babysit my kids for free if I just asked her!"

While she spoke, her eyes brimmed with tears. Mine did, too. Anytime I see someone else's dream surfacing, I'm deeply touched, because I know how sad it is not to be able to live your dream.

Without even taking our order, Sonja slid in next to a

friend at another table to announce that she was going back to school. "I'm going to be a nurse!" she said with tears of joy.

My friend sat across from me, shaking his head. "If I hadn't seen it with my own eyes," he said, "I wouldn't have believed it. Maybe you're right. Maybe everybody *does* have a Big Dream."

You Have a Big Dream, Too!

With whom do you identify in that story? The producer? He thought people with Big Dreams are few and far between. The waitress? She always knew she had a Dream but never felt it was possible.

Every person I meet who is not actively pursuing a Big Dream can identify with one or the other. But the truth is, even those who think Dreams only happen to someone else carry a Dream hidden deep in their heart. And when someone puts a finger on that hidden Dream, the person almost always becomes emotional.

You have a Big Dream, too. God has put a driving passion in you to do something special. Why wouldn't He? You are created in His image—the only person exactly like you in the universe. No one else can do your Dream.

One day when I was teaching this point to some very poor villagers, one of the men suddenly clapped his hands and exclaimed, "That's wonderful news! That means I can stop wishing I were someone else!"

The journey toward your Big Dream changes you. In fact, the journey itself is what prepares you to succeed at what you were born to do.

And until you decide to pursue your Dream, you are never going to love your life the way you were meant to.

Yet millions of people never take the first step.

ANOTHER DAY IN FAMILIAR

What was going through your mind as you read about Ordinary's life of family, friends, and routines? Did it sound...familiar?

It's so easy to get caught up in the demands of life. And we all take refuge at times in routines and recliners and "usual" *anything!*

But if we're just marking time—instead of making a life—we have put our Big Dream on hold. Years pass. Personal losses pile up. We lose our sense of meaning and purpose. We spend our energy unproductively. And the big picture of why God put us on earth in the first place begins to fade from view.

Tragically, a *whole lifetime* can pass without a person ever accomplishing the Great Things he or she was born to do and *wants* to do.

What keeps people from embracing and pursuing their God-given Dreams? I've noticed five common but deadly misconceptions:

- "I don't have a Dream."
- "I have to invent my Dream."
- "I have a Dream, but it's not that important."
- "I have a Dream, but it's up to God to make it happen."
- "I had a Dream, but it's too late."

Take a minute to check your own beliefs. Read each statement carefully. Do any of these describe your beliefs about a Big Dream for your life? (If you're not sure, look at your actions. What you *do* is usually a result of what you actually *believe*.)

But each of these five misconceptions is a trap. If you're caught in one of them, you will never leave Familiar until you reject your wrong thinking and embrace the truth.

So let's look at the truths that can set a Dreamer free.

You do have a Dream. It's part of what it means to be human, created in the image of God.

You don't have to invent your Dream. Like the color of your eyes or your one-of-a-kind smile, your Big Dream was planted in you before you were born. The psalmist David wrote that all the days of his life had been "fashioned for me, when as yet there were none of them."[1]

Your Dream is unique and important. You have been handcrafted by God to accomplish a part of His Big Dream for the world. How? Your Big Dream is meant to fulfill a Big Need he cares deeply about. The reason you're here is to take a part of His Dream from Point A to Point

B. No one else can do it quite like you.

Your Dream is yours to act on. God is waiting for you to value His gift of your Dream enough to live it. He will not force you to choose. Nor will he "make it happen" *for* you. You must choose. You must act. Paul's amazingly productive life was shaped by a single, driving commitment—to "lay hold" of that for which God had laid hold of him.[2]

Your Big Dream is what God has laid hold of you to do.

And fortunately, *it's never too late to act on your Dream!*

Just ask Moses.

"I WILL SEND YOU"

Israel's epic journey to the Promised Land is the story of a nation in pursuit of its Big Dream. Their goal? To reclaim the land "flowing with milk and honey" God had already given them.[3]

But it is also the story of one man, a leader with a Big Dream—a dream to help Israel escape their bondage and find that future. His name was Moses.

You've probably heard or read about the day when God reminded him of his Dream. Moses, then eighty years old, heard his Dream through a burning bush. God said, "I have surely seen the oppression of My people.... I will send you to Pharaoh that you may bring My people, the children of Israel, out of Egypt."[4]

You can imagine Moses' shock. In fact, he responded with one excuse after another.

Did you notice that I said God *reminded* Moses of his Dream to be a deliverer? That's because from birth, Moses had been uniquely prepared and motivated for that very purpose. He knew it; he even thought other Israelites knew it![5] But as a young man, he had pursued it in the wrong way.[6]

Now forty years had passed. I'm sure Moses thought his Big Dream had crumbled to dust.

Then God interrupted Moses' life with an amazing message from the burning bush. It's as if God said, *Your Dream is not dead because the Big Need is still there.*

But how was an aging sheepherder going to rescue an entire nation from the most powerful king on earth? Like all Big Dreams, Moses' assignment seemed far too big.

Here are three insights into every God-given Big Dream that we can glean from Moses' story:

1. A Big Dream always seems overwhelming at first.
2. Ultimately, a Big Dream is aimed at meeting a Big Need in the world.
3. While you still have breath, it's never too late to act on your Dream!

I'm so glad God returns again and again to present us with the gift of our life. Our Dream matters greatly to Him. There's no other you or me, just like there was no other Moses.

Your Dream may not look quite the same as it did
years ago. But the essence of the Dream—the tug of
longing you feel to do what God made you to do—is still
there. No matter what's happened in your past, or what
circumstance you're in, you can turn your heart toward
your Dream, starting now.

CONVERSATIONS WITH THE DREAM COACH

I wish I could visit with you personally, but this book is
our only connection right now. So I invite you to allow
me, in print, to be your Dream Coach. One of my
favorite things to do—yes, it's part of my Dream—is to
help other Dreamers like you move forward on their
journey.

Certain questions come up often, so I'm including a
few here that I have been asked at recent conferences. I
think you'll find these conversations helpful.

> *"Moses was lucky to get his Dream announced to him from a*
> *burning bush. But I haven't had any such experience! I'm in*
> *midlife, and I still can't find my Big Dream. Can you help?"*
> —Lee, Brooklyn, New York

I've known people who can point to one conversation or
spiritual experience when their future suddenly came into
focus. But most of us don't see it all at once. We start with
an inkling, a cluster of interests, a longing that won't go

away. If we start there and set out, we give God a chance to show us more.

One thing I know: God is not intentionally hiding your Dream from you. It's already in you. It's already *who you are.* Your opportunity is to discover it.

These explorations have helped others:

Think back to what you wanted to do while you were growing up. Of course, it might have been a whole list of things. Don't settle for just the job description—a fireman, or movie star, or president. Think about what those roles meant to you then, and what they can reveal about your real interests and motivations now.

Interview three people you respect, who you think are living their Dream. Ask them to share with you why they think you were put on this earth.

If someone came along and gave you all the money you ever wanted, what would you do with it? Probably that's your Dream. Your first answer might be, "Live on a tropical beach and sip pink drinks." Probably the beach only represents the end of your stresses and unfulfillment. It doesn't tell you much about the purpose and fulfillment you would crave once your stresses disappeared.

Observe your life and write down your conclusions. Good questions to ask yourself include:

- What have I always been good at?
- What needs do I care about most?
- Who do I admire most?

- What makes me feel most fulfilled?
- What do I love to do most?
- What have I felt called to do?

Ask yourself what legacy you would like to leave for your children and grandchildren. What do you most want to be remembered for?

"I always wanted to own and run a business that would be successful enough that I could make a positive difference in my country through charity. But life intervened. Now I have a family, a job, and a lot of responsibilities and expenses. Insurmountable circumstances won't allow me to pursue my Dream. What can I do?"
—Kobus, Johannesburg, South Africa

A lot of people feel just like you. Present circumstances make your Dream seem out of the question. But nearly always, the truth is something else. I've found that most people who truly want to pursue their Dream can come up with a plan that makes a beginning possible. Of course, there's a price attached—at least one sacrifice and, often, several.

Most people who feel stuck need to rethink their priorities. Usually they have put a certain standard of living, a way of life, or some other assumption above the priority of pursuing a Dream.

Ask yourself questions like, *What am I willing to*

sacrifice for my Dream? How could I mobilize my family to help me pursue this Dream? To what degree am I using my obstacles as excuses? Is there anything I can do right now to launch me toward my Dream?

The minute you decide that you will do what it takes, you are already in pursuit of your Dream.

∽·

"I come from a family that doesn't seem to believe in Big Dreams. In fact, we were always raised to expect very little out of life and always play it safe. Is that why I feel so afraid to embrace and pursue my Dream?"
—Cyndi, Charleston, South Carolina

So many people come from families—and even whole cultures—that don't believe in Big Dreams. If this is what you experienced, it can be very painful. You feel like you're walking around in a room where the ceiling is six inches too low!

Maybe your family made it clear (without ever saying it) that you're not expected to achieve much. Or maybe your family only approved of certain kinds of Dreams.

I encourage you to spend some time writing out a family Dreams profile of your family. What, in two or three sentences, was the big message about Big Dreams you received as you were growing up? (There is always a message, whether overt or subtle.) Who in your extended family would you say is living his or her Dream? Finally, what consequences do you see in your family because Dreams weren't honored?

Once you understand how your family is affecting your beliefs and choices, you can take steps to change.

GOD LOVES NOBODIES

I wonder if you still feel like a permanent, certified Nobody—unremarkable and unnoticed in your life. If so, I want you to know that God especially *loves* Nobodies!

One of my favorite Nobodies was Agnes Bojaxhiu of Albania. She never went to college, never married or owned a car. But she had a huge Dream: to live out her faith by caring for the dying and the poorest of the poor.

Most of us know Agnes as Mother Teresa, Nobel Prize winner and one of the most admired people of our time. She spent most of her life caring for the poor and dying in Calcutta. But through her Sisters of Charity, her Dream is still touching millions of people around the world.

Whatever you feel is true or not true about you today, you were made to be Someone Special, someone with a Big Dream beating brightly in your heart. And the world is waiting for you to begin your journey.

Once you decide to pursue your Dream, you'll be amazed at how much your life changes.

Remember Sonja, the waitress who wanted to be a nurse? Imagine with me a typical day in her life a few years from now. She will get up in the morning like always—but instead of putting on her apron and dreading another day, she will put on her nurse's uniform. She'll work hard all day doing something she loves. She may even save a life that day. After her shift, she will go home physically exhausted, but happy to the core. She will know that she is living in what I call her "sweet spot"—doing what she loves most and meeting needs at the same time.

Don't wait another day. Tell someone you trust today, "I have a Big Dream." Then, as best you can, tell them what it is. The first time you say your Dream aloud, you will hear your heart say, *You were born for this!*

CHAPTER NINE

LIVING PAST
THE EDGE

*Still trembling, Ordinary picked up his suitcase, turned his
back on Familiar, and walked to the sign. And even though his
fear kept growing, he shut his eyes and took a big step
forward—right through the invisible Wall of Fear.*

And there he made a surprising discovery.

*On the other side of that single step—the exact one
Ordinary didn't think he could take—he found that he had
broken through his Comfort Zone.*

*H*ave you ever been most afraid of doing the very
thing you most want to do? I had that problem, and
it turned me back from my Big Dream time after time.

You see, by the time I got through college, I knew I
wanted to become a creative Bible teacher who could help
a lot of people. That Dream *inspired* me! But to
accomplish my Dream, I would have to stand up and

speak in front of a lot of people. That *terrified* me!

I'd get physically ill for a week before a speaking engagement. Then, when I finally got behind the lectern, I would hold on for dear life, stiff with fright, afraid to move my arms—afraid to move at all! There I'd stand until I had sweated my way through to the last word of my message.

Something had to change.

I knew that if I was ever to hold an audience, I'd have to feel confident enough to move around the platform, use dramatic gestures, connect naturally with my listeners.

As you can probably imagine, my fears raised real questions about my Dream. Was I making a big mistake? And if I was pursuing the right Dream for me, why did I feel so uncomfortable doing it?

You can match my story to Ordinary's. I had embraced my Dream. I had left Familiar, excited to be pursuing it. But soon, I ran into a huge obstacle. Right there, by the sign that said "Leaving Familiar," I hit an invisible Wall of Fear.

And it stopped my Dream in its tracks.

IT HAPPENS TO EVERYONE

You, too, may have taken a big step toward what you really want to do, only to be surprised by a lot of uncomfortable feelings. If so, you probably still remember them. You felt anxious. You felt foolish and full of doubts. You felt exposed, weak, and incompetent. Maybe, like me, you felt so afraid it almost made you sick.

Those feelings may have even turned you around and sent you scrambling right back to Familiar.

What you and I experienced is what happens to everyone who tries to leave his or her Comfort Zone. But I did get past my fear, and you can, too. Let me show you how to understand what's happening—and why—and how to step through that invisible Wall of Fear to experience newfound freedom.

WHEN COZY IS A TRAP

When you think about it, a Comfort Zone ought to be hard to break through—after all, we have spent so much time building it. A Comfort Zone is our cozy quilt of relationships. It's the padding of routines that make us feel good. It's the security fence of acceptable behavior. It's the steel mesh of our past successes and failures.

Our Comfort Zone completely surrounds our life in Familiar, and it feels comfortable.

Inside our Comfort Zone, we feel safe. We're pretty sure we can succeed, look good, and feel happy there. Outside, well, who knows?

Outside everyone's Comfort Zone lies the great Unknown.

That's why we don't want to go there.

Now, there's nothing wrong with a Comfort Zone.

After all, no one likes danger and uncertainty. No one signs up for discomfort.

Yet a Comfort Zone can become a barrier, too. Why? Because our Big Dream always lies outside our Comfort Zone. That means we will have to leave what feels comfortable if we want to achieve our Dream.

Ordinary faced a choice: He could either feel comfort but give up his Dream, or feel fear and pursue it. You might think that if only you were braver or stronger, you wouldn't have to struggle so much with that choice. But every Dreamer does, no matter how talented or brave.

"I WILL BE WITH YOUR MOUTH"

When God described to Moses what he would have to do to fulfill his Dream, the first step was clearly outside his Comfort Zone.[1] "Come now, therefore, and I will send you to Pharaoh," God said.

I can see Moses now—stiffening with fright, reaching for a podium somewhere, anywhere, to hang on to!

"Who am I," he said to God, "that I should go to Pharaoh, and that I should bring the children of Israel out of Egypt?" You can tell that he felt *Unworthy.* Years before, Moses had committed murder, then fled the scene of the crime.

But he also felt *Unable:* "O my Lord, I am not eloquent...I am slow of speech and slow of tongue."

Do you identify with Moses' feelings of reluctance,

fear, and inadequacy? I do. Every Dreamer I've met does. But the great news for Dreamers is that our success doesn't rest only on us.

It's interesting what is revealed in God's answer to Moses. Moses was uniquely chosen for his mission. And Moses was also uniquely gifted. But what mattered more was that God promised to help. He told Moses, "Who has made man's mouth? Have not I, the LORD? Now therefore, go, and I will be with your mouth and teach you what you shall say."

Take a minute to write out a few of the objections— however convincing—that you've come up with for why your Big Dream + Little You = Huge Fear of Failure.

How many of your reasons assume that you're in it all by yourself?

With that in mind, ask yourself, *How might God reply to my personal concerns and fears?*

I remember a woman telling me she was afraid to go ahead with her Dream. When she let the word *unworthy* slip, I said, "Are you waiting until you feel worthy so you can begin?"

"Yes," she said.

My reply startled her. "Well, you aren't worthy," I said. "And you will never feel worthy. If you continue to wait until you feel worthy, you will never live your Dream."

At first this didn't sound like the encouragement she had been looking for. Then a light came on and her eyes widened. What a relief it was for her to put down that false burden! Now she was ready to think clearly about her next step.

You see, every Big Dream is initially way beyond your abilities and experience. We all feel Unworthy and Unable to do a Big Dream. But the Bible says, "God has chosen the foolish things of the world to put to shame the wise, and God has chosen the weak things of the world to put to shame the things which are mighty."[2] God purposely picks Unworthy and Unable Dreamers like you and me!

Now consider this: It's not really your feelings of discomfort, but what you think those feelings mean, that determines what happens next.

BREAKING THROUGH THE WALL OF FEAR

Do you remember all the unwanted feelings Ordinary experienced on the road out of Familiar? At first, things just seemed different. But the farther Ordinary got from the center of Familiar, the more his journey through his Comfort Zone made him anxious and afraid. Finally he was overcome with fear and couldn't take another step.

The closer we get to our own invisible Wall of Fear, the more fear we feel, and the more likely we are to believe a dangerous misconception. Ordinary expressed it this way: "But if I was *supposed* to do this Big Dream, then I'm sure I wouldn't feel so afraid!"

Sounds perfectly sensible, doesn't it? But it's a wrong belief that can trap a Dreamer for years.

Let's state the misconception more fully.

Comfort Zone Misconception #1:
Since I feel fear, my Dream must not be from God.

I can tell you from personal experience how powerful this wrong belief is. For many years, I kept asking God to expand my territory for Him. Looking back, I see that my prayer set a predictable but defeating cycle in motion. It looked like this:

1. *"Please say yes!"* First, I prayed for a larger life for God.
2. *"Yes,"* He answered. His answer was to bring me toward my Dream. But my Dream was always outside my Comfort Zone—doing something I had never done before.
3. *"No!"* I said. I experienced discomfort, anxiety, and often genuine fear. But since I thought that if God was with me, I wouldn't feel fear, I would retreat back to the safety of Familiar.
4. *"Why aren't You saying yes?"* I asked. The next morning would find me on my knees, asking God *again* to expand my territory for Him!

Do you see why I didn't make much forward progress during that time? There was an eighteen-lane freeway that started with me on my knees, led out to the edge of my Comfort Zone, and circled back again.

And I could never figure out why God didn't answer my prayers!

Think back over the times you have attempted to take a big step into new territory. When your fear increased the further you moved toward the Unknown, did you begin to doubt the wisdom of your plan? To wonder if your fear might be a message from God that you were off course?

This misconception leads to a second one.

Comfort Zone Misconception #2:
I can't go forward unless God takes my fear away.

"But *you* could take away the fear," Ordinary cried out. "*Please* take the fear away! If you don't, I can't go on!" His request makes sense. After all, fear is a natural human response to a perceived threat. From the inside, where we're comfortable, fear feels like a barbwire barrier that we should always respect and *never climb over.*

But while some fears—like fear of heights or snakes—can keep us from harm, other fears—like fear of new challenges or the Unknown—will inevitably keep us from our Big Dream.

In my experience, God rarely makes our fear disappear. Instead, He asks us to be strong and take courage. What is courage? As Ordinary discovered, courage is not the absence of fear; rather, it's choosing to act in spite of the fear. You could say that without fear, you can't have genuine courage.

When you do act in courage, you discover that fear doesn't have to stop you. You see that what you thought were your limits are more like starting points.

THE LONGEST SHORT WALK OF MY LIFE

To take courage, you have to decide to go forward *anyway*.

Do you know how I finally took courage and faced my deep fear of speaking in public?

One Sunday, when I was scheduled to speak in a small church outside Dallas, I brought along some black tape. Arriving early, I marked two spots on the platform ten feet away from each side of the podium. Then I asked my wife, Darlene Marie, to sit in the front row and signal to me whenever she wanted me to *step through my Wall of Fear*.

She did not shrink from her duties. I had no sooner grasped the podium in a death grip and started to sweat than she nodded toward the tape mark to my left. That was my cue.

Could I move?

Would I move?

The mark on the floor seemed miles away, but I had decided—and the future of my Dream hung in the balance.

And I did move. "Just a minute, folks!" I said. (At that point, I couldn't walk and speak at the same time!) Then I left the safety of the podium for that black tape. It was the longest and most awkward, unpolished, and panic-filled walk of my life. But my Dream was waiting for me.

As soon as I reached the mark, I started speaking again. But now I felt a surge of freedom. Without that podium to hang on to, I found I could actually move my arms. Make gestures. Lean toward the audience. Keep their attention. And actually enjoy myself.

Now I knew the secret: I didn't have to be afraid of fear. I could step through it—and keep going toward my Big Dream.

Is there a place in your life that you have run away from like I did for years? Are you just a few steps from the Dream you want with all your heart?

Then you need to make a choice. Decide you will stop retreating from fear and step through it instead. Write down your decision, post it, and don't throw the note away until you have taken your first step.

That step through your Wall of Fear is a huge step toward your Dream!

CONVERSATIONS WITH THE DREAM COACH

"I have been fighting my Comfort Zone issues for many years. But I finally decided that I just couldn't do it any longer. Is it ever okay to choose our comfort?"
—Victoria, Toronto, Canada

No one is meant to live under the stress of breaking through their Comfort Zone day after day. But I invite you to ask yourself, *Why is there such a tug-of-war over breaking through this Comfort Zone in my life?* You may never have identified who or what it is you're fighting against.

Your struggle with Comfort Zone issues reveals something important: You really *do* desire your Dream. Otherwise there would be no struggle. You're motivated to get in motion, but your desire to be comfortable stops you. So at this point in your life, comfort is the biggest enemy of your Dream.

There's nothing the matter with wanting to be comfortable. But ultimately, Dreams are to help someone else. Comfort is to help yourself.

One day I realized that my desire for comfort was the enemy of my Dream, and that ultimately my desire for comfort was rooted in my selfishness.

Unfortunately, many people in all walks of life end up making personal comfort their Dream. But it is a false dream, because comfort turns into a prison. How? The more you turn away from your fear, the more you believe that your Comfort Zone is home. And the more time you spend there, the more you become convinced that because you *haven't* stepped through fear, you *can't!*

But let me encourage you. Never think that since you're struggling, your Dream must not be important, or that you're a second-class Dreamer. Just remember that there's no way for any of us to get to the place of our Big Dream without leaving our recliners!

∾

"I have broken through my Comfort Zone in key areas of my life. But I keep finding new areas that I have to deal with if I want to live my Dream. Does the discomfort ever go away?"
—Kenton, Nairobi, Kenya

The truth is, there's always a new Comfort Zone waiting in your future. You'll arrive at many thresholds of discomfort and fear in every Dream. Then, when your Dream expands, like Ordinary's did near the end of the parable, you can expect a whole new set of challenges!

Fortunately, each time you break through a Comfort Zone, the area of your comfort increases. You become comfortable with more and more things. You could stay there, of course, but a Dreamer is a person whose life is in motion.

That black tape on the platform was really just a beginning for me. The next threshold was the next larger church. And the next larger conference center after that. And so on. Then came the day when I was asked to speak to eighty thousand men at the Pontiac Silverdome in Detroit. Did I face fear again on that new edge of my Comfort Zone? Of course! But with the encouragement of friends, the provision of God, and my decision not to run away from my fear, I broke through that barrier.

Hitting the scary edge of your Comfort Zone again and again proves that you're a Dreamer on the move toward your Dream. I tell motivated Dreamers that if they're not encountering a Comfort Zone issue regularly, something is wrong. Maybe they're stuck in Familiar again. Maybe they need to check their pulse!

AN ADVANCE DECISION

You know, it's one thing to wonder what you're going to do next time you face fear at the edge of your Comfort Zone. It's another thing to have already decided! You will immediately benefit from clarity and energy and focus as you pursue your Dream.

My life changed the day I decided to *never again run away from my Comfort Zone fears.* When you think about it, stepping through fear is a small price tag for a Big Dream. That one step—that we face many times in our lives— must be the universal price tag God had in mind. I think God wants to know whether we really want the wonderful gift of His Dream in our life.

So will you make the same commitment I did regarding the Comfort Zone? Will you commit to never again running away from the Wall of Fear at the edge of your own Comfort Zone?

Imagine what your life will look like when you have broken the bondage of fear. You will spread your wings in new ways. You will feel the strength and peace you need to accomplish Great Things. You will move among people and situations with confidence and grace. You will touch many lives in powerful ways. And you will never again retreat from the future you really want.

Your Dream can look that good. And it will.

CHAPTER TEN

UNEXPECTED
OPPOSITION

*Ordinary was speechless and bewildered. He'd heard a rumor
about Border Bullies. But he had supposed that if it were true,
Bullies would be Nobodies he didn't know. He never imagined
they'd be some of the Nobodies who knew him best!*

*Now his Mother, Uncle, and Best Friend all stood
silently before him, blocking his view of the bridge to his
Big Dream. How would he ever get past them? Should he
even try?*

*n*ot long ago, I completed one part of my Big Dream
and began another. Getting the new Dream
launched called for one short drive—from our house to
the airport—then one long flight—from Atlanta, Georgia,
to Johannesburg, South Africa.

Twenty-five years after founding Walk Thru the
Bible, I had decided to resign as president.

Our new Dream was to serve God in Africa. Without a doubt, it was the biggest and most unexpected change our family had ever experienced. Still, I knew it was the right thing to do. My wife and family knew it, too. And God had confirmed it in several highly specific ways.

But the moment the Dream was announced, people started lining up at our front door. They had come to let us know, in the kindest but strongest way possible, that we were *wrong, wrong, wrong!*

"What are you doing? You're at the pinnacle of your career. You have it made! What's the matter with you?"

"The real reason you're leaving has to be that your marriage is falling apart or something is terribly wrong in the ministry. Which one is it?"

"Since many of those who disagree with this are older than you, you must be spiritually deceived. Surely, you are headed toward a disaster!"

"What are you going to do in Africa, anyway? You don't have a business plan. How are you going to support yourself?"

Have you ever met a Border Bully at your front door? Sometimes a Bully is an actual enemy—a Pharaoh who decrees, "I will not let you go!"

But some of the most convincing Bullies you'll ever meet are the people who know and love you. Just seeing them standing in front of you with NO written all over their faces can be quite a shock. What are you supposed to do at a time like that? Do you listen? Do you reason?

Should you agree with them and turn back?

In this chapter I want to help you to understand what's motivating your Bullies when they say things like "No!" and "Turn back now." And I'll show you the wonderful opportunities they have unknowingly carried right to your door.

A RUSH TO THE BORDER

"Turn back" is not what we Dreamers expect to hear at this point in our journey. We've just picked up our new Dream and broken through our Comfort Zone. We're ready to leave. We want to hear people around us say, "Great idea!" "I wish I could do that, too!" or "Go for it!"

So why do we suddenly encounter opposition? Let me try to put this moment in perspective.

In the Comfort Zone, you struggled with yourself—your own self-talk, your own beliefs. You had to make a lonely choice on the road out of Familiar. You had to choose your Dream over your comfort.

But when you enter the BorderLand, you must deal with others. You must confront their words and beliefs. The reason they've suddenly appeared is that now you're disturbing *their* Comfort Zone! That web of relationships and expectations in Familiar is shaking wildly because someone has moved—you.

Each of us has been a Bully to someone else in another situation. We rushed to the Border when a friend or relative was about to do something that would threaten our comfort. Keeping that in mind will help us listen to our Bullies with more understanding.

What have you heard—or said—at the Border of someone's Big Dream lately? See if you recognize any of these opening lines:

"I've given your plan a lot of thought, and I hate to say this, but..."

"Are you sure you're experienced enough for that?"

"That idea of yours is interesting. But where are you going to get the money and the people to make it happen?"

"But we've never done it that way."

Of course, most Bullies mean well. But they catch us at a vulnerable moment. If you're facing Bullies today, be encouraged. The very fact that they're standing in front of you means you're on the move toward your dream. Their opposition can actually help you clarify your dream and strengthen your resolve.

Let me show you how.

WHO'S IN YOUR BORDERLAND?

Fortunately, we meet more people than just Bullies at our Border. Let's take them one at a time.

1. A *Border* Bully *Opposes You*

We've already seen how Bullies work. Remember, they react primarily because you have disturbed *their* Comfort

Zone. They feel threatened. They fear losing something important—their security or routine, their assumptions about success.

Maybe they feel that they're losing *you*. Once I asked a large group of college students who came to mind first when we talked about Border Bullies. Hands shot up all over the place. And nearly all of them had the same answer: "My mom!" or "My dad!"

Ordinary met four Bullies that you might recognize:

- *The Alarmist* says, "It's not safe!" This Bully (Ordinary's Mother) is motivated by fear and tends to exaggerate the risks.
- *The Traditionalist* says, "It's not the way we do it!" This Bully (his Uncle) doesn't like change. He or she often romanticizes the past and is motivated by custom and routine.
- *The Defeatist* says, "It's not possible!" This Bully (Best Friend) sees problems everywhere and is certain that the dream won't and can't happen.
- *The Antagonist* says, "I won't let you!" This Bully (the Landlord) uses authority or intimidation to block your path. Antagonists might come against you because they fear they will lose money or control. Or they may just not like you or what you're doing, and they have the power to stop you.

Who would you identify as a Bully to your Dream? Why do you think this person is against your plans?

2. A *Border* Buddy *Affirms and Supports You*

Most of us have a few Buddies in our lives, and we need them, too. Maybe yours is a good friend, a neighbor, a parent, or a teacher. Buddies care about us and say so. They look on the bright side. They're willing to stand by us—or at least remain neutral—when we come under fire.

Ordinary's Mother changed her mind and became an encourager and supporter for her son. She couldn't help Ordinary get across his Border, but her support helped him on his way.

What people would you identify as valuable Buddies in your life today?

3. A *Border* Buster *Helps You Pursue Your Dream*

A Buster does more than give you support. He or she recognizes your God-given dream and chooses to proactively help you pursue it. In the parable, Champion was a Border Buster. He helped Ordinary understand why his Bullies were so upset. Then he showed him the path of wisdom. Ordinary might have turned back if he hadn't met Champion.

Border Busters in your life are a rare treasure. They're nearly always experienced Dreamers who have been where you are. Often, they enter your life for only a short period— a teacher, for example. Or a boss. Or even a "chance" encounter with a stranger. But you'll never forget them.

Dr. John Mitchell was one of my Busters. He was chairman of the board at the college where I began my teaching career. He could see what I couldn't as a young professor—that my weekends of presenting Walk Thru the Bible seminars to churches around the country were the real direction of my future.

How did Dr. Mitchell champion my Dream? He quietly initiated changes in my teaching schedule so I could spend more time off campus. He told me, "Bruce, some faculty members may be jealous about this arrangement, but I want you to have this. We want you to stay here forever, but I believe God has a big future for you beyond this school. Until then, we'll be a greenhouse for the ministry God is preparing you for."

That's a Dream Champion! He saw things I missed. He believed when I didn't. He made things happen that I couldn't. And he poured courage from his heart right into mine.

Most of us need that kind of help to break through the real obstacle at the Border.

WHO WILL YOU PLEASE?

The single biggest reason Border Bullies stop most of us from pursuing our God-given Dream is our *fear of man.* "The fear of man brings a snare," the Bible says.[1]

It's not easy to stand up against those we love and care about. The urge to be well-liked and admired by others is deeply rooted in our nature.

Yet since almost every Dream is rejected by at least one strong Bully, especially in the early stages, you *will* face a choice. You must decide who you want to please more—your Border Bullies or God.

Is your Dream important enough to you that you are willing to stand and protect it? When you give the right of approval of your Dream to any person or group, you've given them the right to control your Dream.

Now is the time to make choices based on wisdom, not intimidation. Who must you break free from in order to move forward with your Dream? Is there any person or group you are honoring above the Dream Giver?

Once you choose to please God more than others, you are ready to receive from others *only* what is helpful, and move on to the next phase of realizing your calling for God.

VOICES FOR AND AGAINST

Listen to the Border Bullies Moses describes *before he's even met them:* "But suppose they will not believe me or listen to my voice; suppose they say, 'The LORD has not appeared to you.'"[2]

Can you relate? Before you even act, you can hear the anxieties or negative opinions of key people in your life.

As it turned out, Moses was right. The Israelites he was trying to set free feared the Pharaoh's disfavor. Even though they hated their slavery, they didn't want to lose the security of the life they had always known. So they opposed Moses with the very criticism and resistance he expected.[3]

But Moses' most daunting Bully was Pharaoh, the Landlord of Egypt. Pharaoh didn't want to lose this valuable source of free labor. His famous response to their request for freedom: "I will not let you go."

Later, after escaping bondage in Egypt, the nation of Israel faced Bullies again at the border of Canaan. Twelve spies were sent into Canaan to get the lay of the land. When they returned, ten of the twelve said, "Turn back." What lay ahead *was* as promising as God had said, they reported, but to claim the land would be too difficult and too dangerous.[4]

What a sad day in that nation's history! To be within sight of their Big Dream, only to let the opinion of a few Bullies turn the whole nation away.

I hope that as you're reading this, you're gaining new strength for the Dream that's waiting for you. You can get past those negative opinions. You can claim what is already yours.

CONVERSATIONS WITH THE DREAM COACH

Here are some practical ways to deal with the Border Bullies in your life.

"I recently decided to quit my job as a computer analyst to take a lower-paying position with a private health initiative. I want to do something more directly connected with people in need. But the criticism from my family and others has really

set me back. I'm not sure how to process all their opinions.
What do you say to a Bully, anyway?"
—Sanjay, Bangalore, India

Taking a bold step away from financial security and toward the direction of your Dream definitely brings out the Bullies! Here are some key questions that will help you think through their criticism:

Does your Bully have a problem with you, or is it with your Dream? This is an important distinction. Is it you they don't like or trust, or is it something about your Dream that troubles them? Once you identify the source of their concern, you can respond purposefully. Try to separate their questions about your goal from their questions about how you are proposing to reach that goal. You may find, for example, that a Bully could agree with your goal if only you adjusted your timing or the way you're going about reaching your Dream.

What is motivating your Border Bully? Asking this question helps you to identify the kind of Bullies you're dealing with. Are they concerned for you, or afraid for themselves? What do they stand to lose by your action?

Have you clearly communicated your Dream and your plans? Most beginning Dreamers struggle here. We find it hard to see and to state the Dream clearly, even for ourselves. But careful communication has turned a lot of Bullies into Buddies. Keep trying until you can describe what you want to accomplish in one motivating sentence.

Is there merit to their concerns? Border Bullies often

exaggerate the dangers or risks, but they also make important observations. Their opposition can help you to clarify or retarget your plans, especially if they know you or have special knowledge or experience in the area of your Dream.

Listen carefully, asking God for discernment. But don't let anyone but you and the Dream Giver own your Dream!

∽

"What do I do about a very important Bully I can't seem to sway? Should I keep trying to change her mind?"
—Natasha, Moscow, Russia

Much depends on what kind of Bully you're dealing with. Some Bullies you absolutely *have to* convince in order to move forward, especially if it's a boss or a key player in your Dream. If that's the case, be patient. Is it a matter of timing? Is it a matter of helping this person catch the vision? Try to identify what interest of his or hers is most at stake.

If it's a spouse who doesn't agree with your Big Dream, especially over the long term, take it as a caution from God. Before going forward, a husband and wife should be united about any Big Dream that will significantly affect the course of their lives.

Some Bullies simply need to know that you have heard them out. Some need to be affirmed for their viewpoint or role in your life. Some simply need to be avoided.

MAKE YOUR CROSSING

You know you're ready to move past your Border Bullies when you realize that their objections belong to Familiar. But you don't live there anymore.

The Border is the furthest edge of your old life. One more step and you will walk into your new one.

What is that step?

For me and my family, it meant using those airplane tickets. And we did. We made our crossing from Atlanta to Johannesburg—seventeen hours of sitting, waiting, and wondering what lay ahead. But the hard part was behind us.

My experience in the BorderLand taught me that the larger the vision—and the more different it is from what you've done before—the more Bullies will show up to oppose you. But that still doesn't mean you should turn back.

Dwight L. Moody, the innovative nineteenth-century leader, left his mark on the world by going *against* the consensus. About him, Moody's son wrote:

> It may be safely said that in the beginning of all his greatest and most successful efforts he stood alone, acting against the advice of those best able, apparently, to judge of the matter—with the one exception of his most valued human advisor...his wife.[5]

Make your crossing, Dreamer. Your wonderful future is waiting. And the Dream Giver is ready to help you find it.

CHAPTER ELEVEN

DIAMONDS IN THE DESERT

*When the wind finally stopped, Ordinary stood to his feet.
But as far as he could see, there was only sand. The path to his
Dream had disappeared completely. Obviously, his entire trip
through the WasteLand had been a Waste!*

*Hot tears coursed down his dirty cheeks. "You're not a
Dream Giver," he shouted at the sky. "You're a Dream
Taker! I trusted you. You promised to be with me and help
me. And you didn't!"*

*H*ave you ever set out in faith, taking God at His
word, only to run head-on into failure and
despair?

Sometimes when you risk everything, you lose
everything, too.

Or so it seems at the time.

In 1977, soon after Darlene Marie and I started Walk
Thru the Bible in our basement, we began getting

requests for follow-up Bible teaching. A magazine seemed like a natural choice. So we launched a daily devotional magazine called *The Next Meal.*

Our little publishing team felt strongly that God was asking us to proceed on faith. For us, that meant never charging for the magazine, and never asking for money, either.

Our subscription list grew at a phenomenal rate. Testimonies poured in, thanking us for the ministry and submitting names of friends to be added to the list. But the mail brought only meager donations. Still, our contributors and advisors believed that God would honor our commitment. Even our printer said, "Don't worry, Bruce. I know the money will come."

Every month we poured our hearts into it. Every month we waited on God. And every month we sunk deeper into debt. Why wasn't He providing for something we felt certain He had led us to do?

By the fifth month, we had spent all our own funds. We could borrow no more, and we were more than sixty thousand dollars in debt (more than five years' salary for me at that time). Finally, I told our team that if God didn't provide money by the last Friday of the month, we would be forced to stop publication.

Every morning we got on our knees and begged God for the funds to do His work. Then we got up and went to work, full of faith that He would come through.

But He didn't. At five o'clock that Friday, we held a

somber business meeting. Order of business? To stop publication, write painful letters to the printer and our readers, and start working on a plan to pay back every cent of debt, which we did.

The short, hope-filled life of *The Next Meal* was over. As we left the room that night, I told Darlene Marie, "Well, one thing is for sure: God never called us to do magazines, and we'll never do another one!"

But the hurt we felt went deeper than that. You see, we all felt that God *had* called us to do a magazine for Him. We had obeyed Him at great personal cost. And then it felt like God had watched from the sidelines while we went down in flames.

It was one of the most disillusioning seasons of my life. All our efforts had added up to failure and waste. As a result, I lost all confidence that I could ever lead again.

As you might imagine, it didn't take long in that WasteLand for my faith to wither. Before long, I felt adrift in anger and confusion.

"WHAT A WASTE!"

If you have ever endured lengthy trials, or seen an important dream delayed, or felt forgotten by God, you know already how a WasteLand feels. In fact, you might be in a WasteLand of some kind right now. If so, you probably feel like Ordinary did—like your Big Dream has turned into a long, miserable, unfair, complete waste!

I understand. I've been there. But let me reassure you that you're about to read a chapter of great hope.

Every Dream chaser eventually winds up having a desert experience of some kind. When I asked an audience recently how many thought they were currently in the WasteLand, 40 percent of the people raised their hands.

But what so many Dreamers miss during their trek through desert times are the diamonds in the sand—those extraordinary evidences at almost every turn of a generous and merciful Dream Giver at work.

Do you believe me? At the time of my WasteLand experience, I didn't know what I'm telling you now. If I had, it would have prevented a long season of unnecessary pain and wandering.

It wasn't until years later that I could look back on that season and see that God had been faithfully at work. What we couldn't know then was that He had plans for a different kind of magazine, *The Daily Walk,* and He was preparing us to accomplish it. Today, Walk Thru the Bible publishes ten magazines every month, partnering with ministries around the world. (One lesson I learned: Charge for a subscription!)

One hundred million devotional magazines later, it's clear that God didn't let us down. God just had a bigger Dream than we could have achieved or even imagined at the time. And He wanted to grow our faith enough so that we could reach for the Dream with Him.

GIFTS IN THE WASTELAND

Just about every Dreamer I've talked to around the world who has entered the WasteLand is surprised to be there. Why? I've noticed a universal sequence of events.

After we break free of our inner obstacles—our Comfort Zone—and find a way around our outer obstacles—our Border Bullies—we're ready for our Dream to happen. In fact, we feel plenty tested already! We think, like Ordinary, that our Dream is just around the corner.

But most times it isn't. Instead, we encounter a series of unexpected trials that never seem to end. No one prepared us for this. Delays and setbacks drag on. Soon, disappointment sets in. Eventually we begin to think we should abandon our Dream.

Does this sequence ring true in your experience? What could the Dream Giver possibly be doing for our *good* with a plan like that?

I believe our unasked-for desert tests are a series of invitations to grow up—in our understanding of ourselves and of God, and in the strength of our faith in Him.

When the Dream Giver appeared to be "nowhere in sight," Ordinary's faith began to fade. Before Ordinary could fight for his Dream and win, he needed to change on the inside—he needed to learn endurance and trust.

The WasteLand does *not* happen because God isn't paying attention, or because He's angry at us. It doesn't happen because we have sinned (although we can lengthen our time there).

Instead, the WasteLand happens for a good and important reason: It is an invaluable season of *preparation.* It is the place where God transforms you into the person who can do your Dream.

The WasteLand is the Dream Giver's loving gift to Dreamers with a future!

THE IMPORTANCE OF BEING IN OVER YOUR HEAD

I was eating lunch with a friend who has a PhD in leadership development. I asked him, "Based on all your research and experience, what would you say is the most important secret to developing world-class leaders?"

He put his fork down. "Well, it's not a course, a lecture, or a book," he said. He then picked up his fork and started eating again.

His answer intrigued me. I asked him to explain.

"The single best way to develop leaders," he said, "is to take people out of their safe environment and away from the people they know, and throw them into a new arena they know little about. Way over their head, preferably. In fact, the more demanding their challenges, the more pressure and risk they face, the more likely a dynamic leader will emerge."

At first his theory surprised me. It sounded unsafe

and unkind. But on second thought, it reminded me of many of my own experiences in the WasteLand.

In fact, God used a similar approach to raise up a leader in the wilderness, on the journey from Egypt to the Promised Land.

TRAINING FOR GREATNESS

There's just no way to get from Egypt to Canaan without traveling through a lot of WasteLand. Even today, the Sinai Peninsula is one of the emptiest, bleakest places on earth.

Surviving in that kind of terrain changes you. And the Israelites that entered the Promised Land were not the same weak-willed, complaining group that left Egypt. For one thing, almost all of the slave-born generation had died. Only a few remained. After forty years, a new, desert-tested generation had grown up.

One man who saw it all from start to finish was Joshua. During that time of trial and suffering (which he hadn't asked for) and of endless delays (which he'd done nothing to deserve), Joshua matured. He advanced from Moses' assistant to spy and warrior and, finally, to the one person who was fully prepared to lead Israel after Moses' death.

What had the desert years accomplished? When Israel was finally about to leave the desert, Moses told the nation that God had allowed that experience to happen for an important reason: to test and reshape each person from the inside out.[1]

The bottom line of every test in the WasteLand is this: When God seems absent and everything is going wrong, will you still trust God enough to patiently allow Him to prepare you for what's ahead?

I've noticed that the bigger the Dream, the longer the time of preparation. Joseph spent years honing his leadership skills in prison (even though he was innocent) before he rose to rule all of Egypt. David spent years hiding out in desert caves leading four hundred men who were in distress, in debt, or discontented before he was fully prepared to become king.

But like Joshua, Joseph and David passed the tests of the wilderness and emerged prepared for their Big Dreams. And you can, too.

YOUR GIFT COMES WITH A PRICE

God's motive and plan in the WasteLand is to prepare you to become the person who can succeed at your Dream. But the outcome of His actions is up to you. Your response depends on how you answer two important questions:

1. How much do you want your Dream to come true?
2. Do you believe in the Dream Giver enough to trust His purpose and accept His plan of preparation, even if you don't understand or agree with it?

The Bible describes the trials you and I face in the WasteLand as "the testing of your faith":

Count it all joy when you fall into various trials,
knowing that the testing of your faith produces
patience. But let patience have its perfect work,
that you may be perfect and complete, lacking
nothing.[2]

*How can you "count it all joy" when the WasteLand is all you can
see in every direction?* Obviously, the experiences of the
WasteLand don't bring joy. They are painful.

So how can joy live in the desert? Only when we
understand that the reason we are to count it all joy is not
because of the experience, but because of the *result* of the
experience. Look again at this phrase: "that you may be
perfect and complete, lacking nothing."

You see, the WasteLand matures you—if you let it! In
fact, everything you now lack for the upcoming
fulfillment of your Dream is being offered to you in the
WasteLand. God's promise is that you will lack nothing
when you emerge from the other side. When your "lack"
is finished, the WasteLand is finished! That is God's
commitment to you and your future.

And *that's* a commitment that can bring a great deal of
joy, whatever the circumstances.

Not surprisingly, the place we're most likely to
experience testing is exactly where we struggle most to trust
God. Think about the areas where Ordinary was challenged
to trust. Would the Dream Giver provide? Would he guide?
Was he present? Would he keep his promises? Was his plan
the best one, or was there a better one?

These are universal areas of struggle and growth for Dreamers trying to do Big Dreams.

Therefore, you need to make a decision. Will you give God permission to do His work—for as long as He wants, in the ways that He wants, to change you as deeply as He wants—to prepare you for your Big Dream?

It's a huge commitment, but your Dream is worth it. And your decision will open the door to joy in the midst of any circumstance.

So refuse to buy into the lie that your WasteLand is too hard. It's *not* too hard. It's *not* too long. Your tests in the desert are the best answer to one of your deepest desires and prayers: "Please make me into the person I need to be to do the Dream You have created me to do!"

CONVERSATIONS WITH THE DREAM COACH

The most common WasteLand question I'm asked is "What exactly should I do if I'm in the WasteLand?" Here are some suggestions:

1. *Identify* whether you are actually in a WasteLand. Not all trials are WasteLands. Ask yourself if you are already pursuing a Dream or an enlargement of it. The universal experience of the WasteLand feels like delay, waste, inability to make progress, and being pushed past your limits.

2. *Isolate* the main areas where your trust in God needs to grow. What in your Dream do you really doubt God about right now? Ask those around you what they think

God may be trying to teach you. (Then hold on—your friends often have seen it coming before you!) Try to get on God's side of the problem and find ways to invite healthy change.

3. *Install* a few safety nets beneath you to encourage and protect you when you feel like abandoning the call of the Dream Giver on your life. Friends helped me through two long and difficult WasteLand experiences—one in my twenties and another in my forties. Both times I desperately wanted to flee back to Familiar, and both times their counsel and unconditional love kept me steady and on the path to completion instead of desertion.

4. *Increase* the amount of time you spend with the Dream Giver. Devote more time than usual to reading and studying the Bible. Focus on Exodus, Joshua, and Psalms. You'll be amazed how many times you will find the answer you are looking for. Remember to ask God for the wisdom that He promises to give to all who ask in faith. Pray about the specifics that trouble you the most. And keep a spiritual journal. I have filled many Dream Journals during the WasteLand seasons of my life. Like many others, I find that I do best when I can work through my questions, emotions, and insights on paper with my Dream Giver.

5. *Instill* the commitment deep in your heart that you won't turn back, no matter how long or how hard or how painful the path through the wilderness may be.

Hold on to this key truth: "Now the just shall live by faith; but if anyone draws back, my soul has no pleasure in him."[3] Don't turn back in the desert!

THE FAITH-FILLED DREAMER

If we were talking together right now, face-to-face, I could know just by looking into your eyes if you are in a WasteLand. I would recognize the signs of a soul under stress, the traces of pain and disillusionment. But I would also be able to see beyond your circumstances to the stronger, more faith-filled Dreamer you are becoming.

I have spent a number of seasons in the WasteLand. Why? It was the Dream Giver's very best for me—that's all I know for sure. Yet I have a pretty good idea that some of that time I spent there at my own request.

Of course, I didn't *specifically* ask God for more delays, frustrations, and struggles. What I have begged Him for, though, was to enlarge the territory of my service for Him. More service means a larger Dream. And a larger Dream requires a more prepared Dreamer.

More preparation.

More endurance.

More faith.

More settled conviction that no circumstance, difficulty, or turmoil can change the truth of my Dream— or the trustworthiness of my Dream Giver.

Do you, too, long to be a faith-filled Dreamer who's

prepared for all that God has for you and your life? I invite you to join with me in giving Him permission to accomplish that kind of transformation in whatever way He thinks best.

Then turn your heart back toward your Dream, confident that you never again need waste your travels in the WasteLand.

CHAPTER TWELVE

A SURPRISING INVITATION

Walking across the floor of the forest, he felt hushed and small and swallowed up by Greatness.

Then he began to climb. Higher and higher he climbed, following the stream, until suddenly he entered a level clearing filled with bright light.

His heart told him that this was Sanctuary, and he was in the presence of the Dream Giver.

$\mathcal{I}$ remember stepping out of a hot, crowded, noisy house into a Rocky Mountain evening. The door closed behind me. *Click.*

Instantly, the clamor of voices ceased. All my concerns about people and problems faded away. Cool night air brushed my skin. I took maybe five steps across the newly mown grass...and looked up.

Oh!

Stars, stars, and more stars glittered across the inky night sky. The deepest depths of eternity seemed to open above me and around me—silent, immense, waiting.

There I stood in the grip of wonder.

Do you ever remember having a moment like that? The feeling is universal. You suddenly awaken to a deeper dimension. You feel, like Ordinary, "hushed and small and swallowed up by Greatness."

That's what this chapter is about. Somewhere along your journey, it can happen to you—if you choose it. God will ambush you with an invitation to stand in His presence, to come closer, to see further. I call this experience Sanctuary.

In our discussion we'll use quiet words. Words like *invitation, relationship,* and *surrender*. But don't be fooled. Our subject is Greatness—a Great God at work in you to grow both you and your Dream to accomplish Great Things for Him.

Sanctuary is full of surprises. For example, God will offer you invaluable gifts you never thought to ask for. And He will ask for an invaluable gift from you.

Are you ready for the wonder of it?

BESIDE STILL WATERS

Most Dreamers emerge from the WasteLand feeling spiritually and emotionally depleted. Our relationship with God has been tested and, in many cases, damaged by distrust. Often we're in worse shape than we realize.

What our spirits desperately need is time away for comfort, restoration, and transformation.

I wonder if David had just stepped out of his years as a refugee in the desert when he wrote his best-known psalm:

> The LORD is my shepherd; I shall not want.
>> He makes me to lie down in green pastures;
> He leads me beside the still waters.
>> He restores my soul.[1]

Chances are you've had a Sanctuary experience of some kind in your spiritual life already. It might have happened at a retreat, or while you were sitting on a rock looking out over the ocean, kneeling in tears at the front of a church, or deep in a personal quiet time.

Unlike the previous stages of your journey, Sanctuary is an oasis, not an obstacle. It's a pause where you're invited to meet with God to be renewed and to make decisions that will radically affect the rest of your journey.

Before Israel could be ready to invade Canaan, they needed Sanctuary, too.

A NATION'S SPIRITUAL RETREAT

It had been forty years since Israel left Egypt. Now they gathered near the River Jordan, anxious to claim the land flowing with milk and honey.

But first Moses took the people on a spiritual retreat. He reflected on their entire journey. He reviewed the Ten Commandments and their covenant with God. And he led them through repentance and recommitment. Listen to his emotional appeal:

> "I have set before you life and death, blessing and cursing; therefore choose life, that both you and your descendants may live; that you may love the LORD your God, that you may obey His voice, and that you may cling to Him, for He is your life and the length of your days; and that you may dwell in the land which the LORD swore to your fathers...to give them."[2]

You see, their long journey had brought the children of Israel to a place of decision. A choice. Would they choose to love God and place Him first in their hearts— or not? That choice is at the heart of each of the three encounters waiting for a Dreamer in Sanctuary.

These encounters last different lengths of time and occur in a specific order. And each encounter is a prerequisite for the life-changing event that follows.

Yet each one is only an invitation. That means it's optional. You can say yes and proceed. Or you can say no and look for a detour.

But what you say and do here will determine the future of your Dream.

THREE INVITATIONS

In the parable, Ordinary awoke by a stream and heard an invitation from the Dream Giver to come to His Sanctuary. So Ordinary followed the stream into a forest. In a clearing filled with light, he found a pool of still waters and sensed there the Dream Giver's presence.

When you enter Sanctuary, the first call you hear will invite you to leave behind the dirt and hurt of the WasteLand.

"Come to the water."

God will ask you to come into His presence for rest and restoration—physical, emotional, and spiritual. Water is a universal symbol of refreshment and new life. God wants to restore you, inside and out. And after the WasteLand, you'll *need* it! "When Ordinary emerged from the pool, the last traces of the WasteLand had been washed away."

Sanctuary is a special time in your life. And it will change you. But sometimes we don't heed God's invitation to rest—and He has to press it upon us. I remember a time when sickness forced me to slow down and receive the restoration I desperately needed.

The water of restoration prepares you for what comes next.

God will then invite you into closer relationship with Him.

"Come into the light."

But if you're like many, you might resist the invitation to come into the light, even as you're longing to accept it. During a recent Sanctuary experience, I felt more drawn by God's love than ever before—but also more exposed. My flaws and sins had never seemed so obvious and unattractive.

Please don't turn away from His invitation! The Bible says, "God is light and in Him is no darkness at all."[3] Allow God's light to enter those dark areas of your life. It's a wonderful and humbling experience. Ask for and accept His love, forgiveness, and healing.

Only after cleansing is real communion possible. But that is true in any relationship. Once past wrongs are dealt with and resolved, a friendship can reach new depths.

When your relationship with God deepens into a genuine trust in His character, you will be ready for the final invitation.

"Come higher."

Now God will ask you to consecrate yourself to Him—and surrender your Dream.

When Ordinary heard the Dream Giver's request, he was shocked. Give back his Dream now, after all the hardships he had faced on his journey? Now, when he could finally see his Big Dream shining brightly on the horizon? On his whole journey from Familiar, Ordinary had never held his Dream more tightly than he did at that moment. And now the Dream Giver wanted him to let it go.

What a moment this is in a Dreamer's journey! What God asks feels so *impossible*. If you've already come to this place in your journey, you know I'm not exaggerating.

IDENTIFYING THE REAL OWNER

I'll never forget a night in Des Moines, Iowa, when God made a seemingly impossible request of me. Darlene Marie and I had been asking God to show us what was next for us. That night I found myself praying, "Lord, we've come so far. What is next?"

"Give Me your children," was His answer.

At first, I was too shocked to respond. Then I said no, and I was plunged into hours of turmoil.

I wrestled with God until 3 A.M., when I was finally able to release my beloved children and my wife completely into God's care. It was a painful—but completely freeing—surrender. Since that day, my family no longer belongs to me, but to God. They are simply His gift to me, to love and cherish.

If you're a parent, you especially understand my intense struggle that night. The things we love the most, we hold most closely, don't we?

In another such experience, God put His finger directly on my Big Dream. For years I had struggled to give back to God what I understood to be my life's work— the growing ministry of Walk Thru the Bible. Then the day came when I felt absolutely sure He was asking me to implement a financial policy that would end the ministry.

Looking back now, I see that I was holding far more tightly to the gift of my Dream than to the Dream Giver Himself.

I hesitated. I questioned. I rationalized. I prayed and prayed. Finally the moment came when I surrendered the Dream called Walk Thru the Bible on the altar. I made the decision I knew was right, informed our team, and drove home, sure that the ministry would soon close its doors.

When I got home, I told Darlene Marie that, as far as I could tell, this chapter of our life was over. Forced to choose between God and my Big Dream, I had chosen God.

But Walk Thru the Bible did not close. Instead, God opened many new doors and amazing opportunities.

HE GIVES YOU SOMETHING BETTER

As you think about Sanctuary, would you say it describes where you are right now? If you say yes, you're facing one of three specific invitations:

1. *Will I allow God's love to bring rest and restoration to my body, mind, and soul?*

2. *Will I allow God's light to shine in my heart, and then move forward from cleansing into communion?*

3. *Will I give my Big Dream back to the Dream Giver, no strings attached?*

Each of these invitations is rich with possibility and promise. But the third invitation—to surrender our Dream to God—is the most difficult to accept.

Surrender isn't a one-time event. In my experience,

we surrender other, smaller Dreams throughout our lifetime. That might include possessions, expectations, a career, a hobby, a standard of living, or a personal loyalty—whatever comes between our Dream and its fulfillment.

But the time will come when God asks you to surrender the Dream itself. Often, He'll ask you to take a very tangible step to seal your decision. That could be selling or giving something away, signing a contract, moving, or even resigning.

Of course, you don't *have* to give your Dream back. Remember, every choice in Sanctuary is an invitation. And the truth is, a huge majority of Dreamers choose to keep their Dreams. But consider what's at stake.

If you don't surrender your Dream, you will be placing it higher on your priority list than God. You will go forward from this moment with a break in your relationship with your Dream Giver. Your Dream will become your idol.

But your Dream—no matter how big—will make a tiny god. Your Dream is meant to be about more than itself or you. A God-given Dream brings you together with what God wants to do in His world *through you.* You are meant to be a river of blessing, not a puddle drying in the sun.

You probably know a Dreamer-owned Dream when you see one. They're everywhere. They're always smaller and more selfish than the Dream Giver intended. They get corrupted. They make people "successful" but not fulfilled. They build the reputation of a person but often bring dishonor to the Dream Giver. They do as much harm as good—and sometimes a lot more.

Let me ask you something. Have you come this far, and learned so much about the Dream Giver's character and desires for you, only to settle for *that*?

George Mueller, who was "father" to many thousands of orphans in nineteenth-century England, said, "Our heavenly Father never takes anything from His children unless He means to give them something better." I agree!

Therefore, Dreamer, I challenge you to unconditionally release your Big Dream to God. Put it in His hands and walk away. I'm not talking about a symbolic surrender, but a real one. The longer you've fought for your Dream, the harder your choice will be. But God understands exactly what you've been through and how you feel.

Remember who He is and what He has proven true about Himself in your life. Then obey. Choose to put the Giver before His gift in your life.

It may feel like the biggest step of faith you have taken so far. But it will open the door to a *God-sized* Big Dream in your future.

CONVERSATIONS WITH THE DREAM COACH

"If God loves me so much, why doesn't He just give us more power to accomplish our Dream, instead of asking us to give it back?"

—Augusto, São Paulo, Brazil

It's so important to know that God cares about *you* even more than your Dream! And what He wants most with you is a thriving relationship. So I encourage you to receive His love with confidence. You'll find, as many have, that it's only as you spend more time communing with God that you can do more for Him.

But relationship with God is about a lot more than warm feelings. Just ahead is the Valley of Giants, and God is preparing you to succeed there. If you don't trust Him with your Dream now, you'll probably fall to Unbelief when you face your Giants.

"You said that the choices in Sanctuary are optional, and that many Dreamers turn away. That means a Dreamer can just go forward with her Dream and never deal with sin problems. How might this choice affect the future of her Dream?"
—Marita, Manhattan, New York

You can refuse to do business in Sanctuary and still continue to pursue your Dream, but you will never be or achieve all God had in mind for you. We all deal with sin problems. But ongoing, major, unconfessed sin will keep you from what God wants for you.

Of course, God isn't shocked when a Dreamer shows up in Sanctuary still dragging around a long list of unfinished business. The truth is, when we first started out toward our Dream, we couldn't see some of the dark areas in our life that are so obvious now.

But don't go on making compromise after compromise when you can come freely into His light. There's no such thing as a truly successful Dream apart from a cleansed Dreamer.

THE WORLD-CHANGERS AMONG US

If you are in Sanctuary today, you are in a very promising place. You can proceed as eagerly as Ordinary did toward what God has for you. What's waiting for you there is a new Dream as big as God's Dream for the world.

There is something memorable about a Dreamer who has come through Sanctuary. All the leaders I admire most have been through Sanctuary many times. They have a quiet influence and depth that others don't. It comes, I believe, from spending a lot of time in the Dream Giver's presence—after walking away from lesser Dreams along the way.

But Great Things aren't just the legacy of unusually gifted Great Men and Women. Great Things are what *you will accomplish* when you put God first and make Him owner of all you care about most.

Greatness is your real future. Are you ready for the wonder of it?

CHAPTER THIRTEEN

THE HEART OF
A WARRIOR

*In the morning, Ordinary entered a broad valley that seemed
to lead up to the high country. The Land of Promise was near.*

*Soon he came upon a sign that read: "Beware,
Dreamer! Valley of the Giants!"*

*Ordinary stared at the sign. So the returning Dreamers
were right. Giants were real.*

*What should he do? He had no weapons. He had no
plan. But his Big Dream was bigger than ever. And he trusted
the Dream Giver.*

So he decided to press on.

When you first set out on your journey, Giants are
the last thing on your mind. You know you're born
for a Big Dream, not big fights.

I'm sure a young shepherd named David didn't think
he was born to take on a Giant. Not even after he had

killed a lion and a bear. Not even after the prophet
Samuel had appeared at his parents' home to anoint him
for God's amazing Dream for David's life—to grow up to
be king.[1]

But one afternoon, there he stood, a mere teenager and
the only person in Israel who couldn't *not* take a stand against
the enormous, oppressive, God-dishonoring Goliath.

While two armies watched in amazement, David
walked out to meet his Giant. "I come to you in the name
of the Lord of hosts!" he shouted. "This day the Lord will
deliver you into my hand!"

Then he put one small stone in his sling and *ran
straight toward Goliath.*

Moments later, the stone found its mark. The Giant
came crashing down.

That stunning victory over a Giant accomplished so
much. It brought fresh hope to Israel's Dream of freedom
from oppression. It opened the Israelites' hearts to a boy
who was born to be their king. And it brought great
honor to God.

This chapter is about Giants and how to bring *yours*
down.

If you're looking up at a Giant today, I want to
encourage you. You haven't made a mistake or taken a
wrong turn. You're not staring defeat in the face. In fact,
you'd be foolish to turn back!

Why? Because your Giant is strong evidence that
you're right on track to achieve the Big Dream God put in
your heart.

THE MANY FACES OF GIANTS

A Giant is a very real and completely overwhelming obstacle you encounter on the road to your Dream.

Overcoming a Giant requires you to use everything you've learned so far on the journey to your Dream, including courage, wisdom, trust, endurance, and surrender to God. You will need God's power to overcome a Giant, and sometimes you'll need one miracle after another.

Since your Dream is unique, the Giants you face will be unique to you, your circumstances, and your Dream. See if you recognize any of these Giants:

A lack of resources. You don't have the power, finances, resources, connections, schooling, or opportunities you need to make your Dream happen. If that critical need isn't met, you can't advance. And you see no solution in sight.

An immovable system. You must find your way through the maze of a bureaucracy or legal system, but you can't even find the front door.

An opposing group or individual. People with the means to help make your Dream happen, don't. Or they work actively against you. Perhaps you face racial or social prejudice that seems to put your Dream out of reach.

An intimidating circumstance. This is a situation that is beyond your control. For example, your Dream is in New Jersey, but your husband gets transferred to Tokyo. Or you can't pursue your Dream because you must care for an invalid family member.

A *crushing physical or spiritual burden.* Your opportunity is limited by an illness, physical challenge, or addiction. Or you face a spiritual issue of some kind that prevents you from going forward.

Take a moment to consider the Giants you have faced so far in your life. Can you list them? How did you get past them, if you did?

Now let me ask you, when you have faced a Giant in the past, did you believe that God would help you? And did He?

These are important questions. Unless you believe God will show up, you're very unlikely to defeat (or even fight) a Giant. That's why the Commander told Ordinary, "Unbelief is much more dangerous to your Dream than any Giant!"

As Israel discovered, unbelief and rebellion can derail a Dream for years.

A MOST UNUSUAL BATTLE PLAN

Of the twelve handpicked spies sent into Canaan, do you really think ten were cowards? I don't. I think they looked at the walled cities, highly trained armies, and Giants in the Promised Land, and they came back to Moses with a sensible report: *The enemy is very strong. We seem weak by comparison. Therefore, we should not attack.*

But while their military assessment may have been well-thought-out, their faith had failed them completely. Joshua and Caleb wanted to advance, but the other ten spies feared the Giants more than they trusted God. Their arguments sent a nation spiraling into Unbelief, and they turned back to the desert.

It was a terrible defeat for Israel's Dream, and they wasted the next forty years wandering in the desert.

Of course, when Israel returned after four decades to try again, the same Giants still blocked their progress. But this time Israel rejected fear and chose to trust God. Now they were ready to move forward under the direction of the Dream Giver, who promised, "Every place that the sole of your foot will tread upon I have given you. I will not leave you nor forsake you."[2]

But God deals with Giants differently than we do, and His plan for conquering Jericho was quite a surprise. He told Joshua that the people were to attack the city by simply walking around it. Then, at just the right time, they were to blow trumpets and shout. If Israel did exactly as He said, the walls of Jericho would fall down.

Can you imagine the courage it took General Joshua to tell his army that he planned to conquer a city by walking around it and making a lot of noise? Joshua risked rejection and humiliation as a leader, while Israel faced total defeat.

Has God ever asked you to take a big risk, to face a Giant for your Dream? When He does, something important is at stake. Because, as you'll see, your Giant exists in the first place because God is up to something larger than you, larger than your Dream, larger even than a victory.

What is that purpose? If God has the power to part the sea with a rod or knock a city down with a shout, why doesn't He use all that power to remove our Giants once and for all?

THE REASON FOR GIANTS

For a long time, I searched for the answer. But it eluded me at every turn.

Then one day I realized I had been looking up at Giants from my perspective—and not down on them from God's!

The occasion was a conference for several hundred Dreamers in South Africa. I was in the middle of presenting, statement by statement, a list of what God had said about why He sometimes chose to perform miracles to defeat Israel's Giants.

Suddenly a pattern of truth emerged, a pattern I had somehow missed before. Look at the recurring message in these verses:

"Then you shall know that I am the LORD your God who brings you out."[3]

"That you may know that there is none like Me in all the earth."[4]

"That My name may be declared in all the earth."[5]

"That you may tell in the hearing of your son and your son's son the mighty things I have done in Egypt...that you may know that I am the LORD."[6]

"I will gain honor over Pharaoh. Then the Egyptians shall know that I am the LORD."[7]

"That all the peoples of the earth may know the hand of the LORD, that it is mighty."[8]

None of us at that conference could miss the message. Do you see it, too?

God wants to be known and honored for who He is. Giants are the primary opportunity to make His power and goodness known to a doubting world. And when He chooses to defeat a Giant through a miracle—that is, an event that cannot be explained in any way other than "God did that!"—He receives all the glory.

The conference came to a halt. We put aside the Dream Giver notebook. We felt a tremendous need to change our thinking about our Giants. Then and there we asked God's forgiveness for how our wrong thinking had led us to run away from Giants in the past.

I led us in a heartfelt prayer of new commitment: "Dear God, forgive us for running from the Giants that stand in front of us. Never again will we run from our Giants. Please send us the Giant of Giants, because we want to bring You the very greatest glory possible!"

Now let me ask you this: Do you need to radically revise your beliefs and attitudes about Giants? Are you ready to seek out your biggest Giants and come against them as a Warrior for God's glory? Are you ready to seem ridiculous, take risks, feel weak and small so that God's power and goodness will be made clear to all?

If you have been moving *away* from what He wants for you instead of toward it, tell God that you won't ask Him to remove your Giants anymore. Instead, you will advance *toward* every Giant between you and your Dream.

CONVERSATIONS WITH THE DREAM COACH

*"I want to take a risk of faith, but I don't know what to do.
What does a risk actually look like?"*
—Celia, Miami, Florida

You take a risk when something important is at stake—
and you might lose—but you decide to move forward for
God. David took a risk in going out to battle Goliath. For
you, it might be a phone call or a public commitment.

A risk of faith takes you toward your Dream, even if it
doesn't feel comfortable to you. One risk I've taken lately
is to take a stand against corruption in Third World
nations. I risk losing favor with those in power who profit
inappropriately. But I am determined not to retreat from
that greedy Giant.

❧

*"Our elder board seems blinded by Unbelief about what we
could do in our community. How can I help us focus on what
God wants done, and not on our doubts and limitations?"*
—Greg, Los Angeles, California

Unbelief sets you up for defeat before you even start. I
experienced this while leading a group that was trying to
defeat a massive community Giant. It overwhelmed the
group's Dream and our individual Dreams, too. Hope was
draining away by the minute.

Then I suggested we stop thinking about the Giant
and start listing aloud the miracles of the Bible. By the

time we had named twenty-five, our Giant had shrunk dramatically and our faith had grown greatly. Our renewed hope in God completely turned the meeting around.

REACH FOR YOUR STONE

The Bible says that "the eyes of the LORD run to and fro throughout the whole earth, to show Himself strong on behalf of those whose heart is loyal to Him."[9]

The Dreamers I know who are changing the world know a secret: God is eager to show Himself strong toward Dreamers who take risks to do what He wants done. Are you ready to witness firsthand that kind of power at work in your world? I think so.

I hope this chapter has encouraged you to value the great opportunities awaiting you in your Valley of Giants. There are so many Goliaths in our world, and so few Davids. You are called to take a stand for the Dream Giver, alone if necessary. But the rewards are great. So don't back down. You *are* a Warrior.

Your Dream lies in the direction of an overwhelming obstacle. If you go toward it today, you will bring God honor. And you will experience a life marked by miracles as God intervenes on your behalf.

That Giant rising up in front of you right now is roaring defiance against humanity, against you, against God's Dream for His world.

Warrior, isn't it time you reached for your stone?

CHAPTER FOURTEEN

LIVING OUT YOUR BIG DREAM

One day, Ordinary took a stroll near the city gates. As he walked, he talked with the friendly Anybody children who followed him.

Then he heard the Dream Giver say, What do you see?

Ordinary stopped. He looked down into the children's faces. "I see beautiful Anybodies in great need," he said.

Yes, *said the Dream Giver.* What else do you see?

Then Ordinary looked up. He could hardly believe his eyes. Carved on the inside of the gate was the Name of his Dream!

Your Big Dream lies here, *the Dream Giver said.*

We stepped off the plane on the other side of the globe, happy to have finally arrived in our Land of Promise.

Johannesburg is a beautiful city on a plateau in southern Africa. Under the streets lie the world's richest deposits of diamonds and gold. But above, in the streets, there is great need.

We rolled up our sleeves and put our shoulder to a growing list of ministry and humanitarian projects in southern Africa. We developed training resources and conferences for leaders and pastors. We made inroads with leaders and presidents in several countries in Africa. And we partnered with a large AIDS response movement.

But the need that stole our heart was the plight of the children.

Across southern Africa, the AIDS epidemic has left more than thirteen million children with neither father nor mother. Every day, eight thousand people in sub-Saharan Africa die of AIDS, while another fourteen thousand contract the HIV virus for the first time.

Like Ordinary, we may have been expecting our Dream to look different from this picture of death, dying, and loneliness—something other than the biggest Big Need we had ever seen. Maybe we were expecting to hear, "Congratulations, Dreamers! You have arrived!"

But what we heard instead was the Dream Giver's gentle question, *What do you see?*

And what we saw broke our hearts.

But thankfully, we encountered more than just suffering and cruel statistics. We found that the great needs of this continent matched our deepest desires to make a difference in this world. Now every day we feel a growing desire to pour our passions, abilities, and effort into this Dream.

In this last chapter, I want to share a snapshot or two from my personal journey. Consider this a letter home from Bruce "Ordinary" Wilkinson in the Land of Promise.

The stories are ours, but I hope you see your life in every word. Not the location, necessarily, or even the direction of my work, but the picture of a completed Dream—yours—that is waiting to come true.

If you're doing your Dream right now, hopefully you will find insights on how to accomplish even more for God in your Land of Promise.

And if you haven't realized your Dream yet—even if you haven't left Familiar—then I hope to show you how urgent it is for you to reach for your destination now with all your heart.

TINY DROPS OF HOPE

How does a person begin to understand the reality of thirteen million orphans?

Maybe like this: Put the populations of Los Angeles and New York City together. Let that combined metropolis be made up of only needy children. In that whole city, let there be not one mother or father. Let there be a ramshackle home where a nine-year-old boy is the head of the household. Let his six-year-old sister leave home every morning to look for food.

Now let these children be yours.

As we began to see firsthand the orphans' needs, our Big Dream began to look like a nightmare.

Night after night we prayed, "Lord, show us what we can do!" We began by doing what we could. We gave away money. We gave away clothes. We visited "families" of children living in tin shacks.

But our efforts were like tiny drops of hope in an ocean of suffering.

At the request of the president of Kenya, we began work on *Beat the Drum,* a major motion picture about the AIDS crisis in Africa. The film follows a boy named Musa on a journey from his village, where both of his parents have died, to the city, where he hopes to find a living relative.

One day we were to shoot a scene on a street corner in Johannesburg. But when the sixty-person crew arrived at the set that morning, the real story was already there waiting.

Police officers stood around filling out forms. In the night, a boy Musa's age had died on the sidewalk, a casualty of hunger and exposure. No one knew his name or where he was from.

The crew worked in tears all day on our film about Musa, shaken but determined that the nameless orphan had not died in vain.

That night over dinner with friends, Darlene Marie and I heard about a couple who owned a farm to the north of us. Every morning at sunrise, orphans gathered at their front gate to ask for food. The couple responded as generously as they could. They knew that if they didn't, some of the children they turned away would die.

Word had spread quickly. The number of hungry children swelled to hundreds every morning. Still the farm couple refused to turn them away. Before long, they had given away all their food and produce, and used up their savings to buy more.

Their noble sacrifice finally ended when the wife had a nervous breakdown and the couple moved away.

Darlene Marie and I went home that night in distress. Clearly, the scope of our response to the needs of orphans didn't begin to match the scale of the problem.

DO NOT HIDE YOURSELF

Not long after, my son, David, was driving me through a poor township where he had been spearheading an antipoverty initiative. I was struck by all the children roaming the streets. At so many corners, new ones would run up to our windows, seeking food.

I turned to my son and asked a question that would change the course and size of my Dream: "What does God want done with the orphans?"

David's answer was intuitive and almost immediate. "God wants these orphans to be loved and cared for," he said. "He wants them to have food and a home."

As he was speaking, words I had read recently in the book of Isaiah pierced my heart. I reached for my Bible, and I read aloud:

Is it not to share your bread with the hungry, and
that you bring to your house the poor who are cast
out; when you see the naked, that you cover him,
and not hide yourself from your own flesh?[1]

The answer was inescapable. We *did* know what God
wanted done. And we could not—we must not—hide.
I went back to the text and read on:

Then your light shall break forth like the
morning, your healing shall spring forth speedily,
and your righteousness shall go before you; the
glory of the LORD shall be your rear guard. Then
you shall call, and the LORD will answer; you shall
cry, and He will say, "Here I am."[2]

God had promised to provide, to protect, to answer,
to always be with us. How then could we say no to what
He wanted done?
We had been asking the question "What can we do?"
But it had brought inadequate results. Now we saw that
every Dreamer is invited to look at a Big Need through
God's eyes, then ask, "What does God want done?"

TURN THE TIDE

We began to strategize in a new way. The size of the Need
would become the size of our Dream.
Therefore, we refused to start with the resources at

hand or what we *thought* we could succeed at. Instead, we started with what needed to be done—no matter how intimidating—and worked toward a plan from there.

It wasn't long before a major opportunity presented itself. We sponsored a five-day Turn the Tide conference to train pastors, leaders, and laymen. The conference was linked by satellite to churches and organizations all over southern Africa. Over the course of the conference, I shared my heart about the orphans. And I presented a plan that our team had developed, called Turn the Tide for Children, to work with churches and faith-based initiatives throughout Africa.

But my challenge to the conferees was specific. I was asking this group to sponsor one thousand orphans at 150 rand (about twenty dollars) each per month. The most orphans to be sponsored previously in one meeting was three hundred, I'd been told, but that had been in the United States. This was Africa. I told the audience that if we could find sponsorships for one thousand orphans, we would all *know* it was God at work!

Then I raised the stakes. "And I'm praying for one family here to sponsor another thousand."

The audience gasped.

But when the numbers were all in, one thousand orphans had been sponsored. Then a family came forward to say they had wanted to do something for orphans for a long time. They would sponsor one thousand by themselves. Applause broke out across the audience and at downlink sites across Africa.

We had taken God's Big Dream for orphans to heart. And He had kept His promise in an astonishing way.

But the day wasn't over. After the service, I was having a cup of coffee when three men walked up. The Lord had spoken to them, they said. The company they owned would sponsor another thousand children.

Three thousand sponsorships in one day! It was an exciting beginning.

Our Dream for orphan care—along with many other ministry and humanitarian initiatives—continues to grow. Turn the Tide for Children has started to plan for a massive network for proven organizations, faith-based movements, churches, and orphanages all across Africa. Our Dream is that each orphanage will have a school, a self-sufficient farm with livestock, training in biblical values, mentoring, and equipping in business. The next generation of African leaders is going to rise up from these millions of orphans as Dreamers who will slay the great Giants of the continent.

But time is running out. In Botswana, just three hours north of where we live, four out of every ten adults are dying of AIDS. Churches, agencies, and willing families in the region cannot keep up with the need.

Still, I believe we are going to see one of the greatest miracles in modern history. Why? Just look at the size of our Giants! And dedicated Warriors are rising up and attacking them.

WILL YOU BE MIGHTY?

Why did that nameless boy die on the sidewalk? I believe his Need was someone else's Dream—a Big and important Dream that had not been embraced and pursued.

That's a sobering conclusion, I know.

Yet it certainly cannot be God's will that any child die alone and abandoned. Surely God placed a particular set of interests and abilities in one person, somewhere in this world, and put that person in a time and place where Great Things could happen—*should* have happened—for that boy.

Will you take up the challenge that so many have avoided?

Even after their big victory at Jericho, it took Israel many years to conquer the land of Canaan. Their commission was to conquer, divide, and settle in *all* the land. But the nation's faith ran out before their Dream was fully realized. Many pockets of Israel were never conquered.[3]

But two Warriors, Joshua and Caleb, purposefully put themselves out on a limb in pursuit of God's Big Dream. They initiated great acts of faith to claim more territory for Him. I call them Mighty in Faith.

Take Caleb, for example. Most of Israel was already settling down to life in Familiar when Caleb decided to attack a hill city everyone else had avoided. He told Joshua:

Give me this mountain of which the LORD spoke
in that day; for you heard in that day how the
Anakim were there, and that the cities were great
and fortified. It may be that the LORD will be with
me, and I shall be able to drive them out."[4]

Do you see the uncertain outcome Caleb was willing
to risk because He trusted completely in God's word?
Giants and fortified cities did not change God's promise
in the least.

A third Warrior comes to mind who was Mighty in
Faith. His name was Jabez. During the era that followed
Joshua and Caleb, Jabez prayed, "Oh, that You would
bless me indeed, and enlarge my territory."[5] And the Lord
answered his prayer.

Could it be that God honored Jabez's faith-filled
prayer because this man was still living out the commission
of Joshua to take *all* the land for God? I think so.

Will you be a mighty man or woman of faith?

Ask yourself, *How big is my whole territory? What would
happen if I made the size of my territory (or need) the measure of my
effort? How would that change the way I approach living out my
Dream?*

"LET ME SHOW YOU MORE"

Just when Ordinary began to feel that his Dream was
finally accomplished, the Dream Giver said, *Let me show you
more.*

Friend, there's so much more ahead for you, too. I wonder how you will respond when that still, small voice comes to tell you it's time to leave Familiar once again.

I hope you reach for your new life with confidence. So many Dreamers do not. Once they've accomplished a Dream, they settle in to enjoy and try to "own" it. But Dreams don't work that way. They turn in on themselves and, eventually, become just another little empire of the self.

But you were born for more. You are called to go after larger and larger Dreams for God. And He will go with you.

So when you hear Him say, *Come further,* pick up your knapsack. Your horizon is full of promise. Another Big Dream is out there waiting for you, and if you don't pursue it, something important won't happen.

I wrote this book to help you on your journey—to send you my feather. My prayer is that it will help lead you toward miracle after miracle for His glory.

A Closing
Invitation

ife isn't meant to be impossible to understand. We should be able to recognize God's fingerprints in our lives. It is then up to us to decide whether we will cooperate with what He is doing, both in our hearts and in our world. God has given you a Big Dream. I hope this book has convinced you to chase after that Dream with every fiber of your being.

As I meet people around the world, there's nothing I love more than hearing remarkable and even miraculous stories from those whose lives have been changed by what they have learned. And if this book has encouraged you to take the next step toward realizing your Dream, please write and tell me about it. I would love to hear about your Dream!

Of course, living your Big Dream is much more complex and challenging than can be described in a 160-page book. Visit us at www.TheDreamGiver.com to find additional coaching tools and resources, including a daily e-mail from me about pursuing and living your Dream.

I look forward to hearing from you.

Now may you devote yourself to His Dream for you. And may heaven describe you as one of those rare people who live to achieve Great Things for the glory of God.

Notes

CHAPTER EIGHT
1. Psalm 139:16.
2. Philippians 3:12.
3. Exodus 13:4–5.
4. Exodus 3:7–10.
5. See Acts 7:25.
6. See Exodus 2:11–25.

CHAPTER NINE
1. You can read the story in Exodus 3–4.
2. 1 Corinthians 1:27.

CHAPTER TEN
1. Proverbs 29:25.
2. Exodus 4:1.
3. See Exodus 5:20–21.
4. See Numbers 13:17–33.
5. W. R. Moody, *The Life of Dwight L. Moody* (Westwood, NJ: Barbour and Company, 1985), 430–431.

CHAPTER ELEVEN
1. The whole book of Deuteronomy is the text of Moses' message to the people of Israel.
2. James 1:2–4.
3. Hebrews 10:38.

CHAPTER TWELVE
1. Psalm 23:1-3.
2. Deuteronomy 30:19–20.
3. 1 John 1:5.

CHAPTER THIRTEEN
1. See 1 Samuel 16–17.
2. Joshua 1:3, 5.
3. Exodus 6:7.
4. Exodus 9:14.
5. Exodus 9:16.
6. Exodus 10:2.
7. Exodus 14:17–18.
8. Joshua 4:24.
9. 2 Chronicles 16:9.

CHAPTER FOURTEEN
1. Isaiah 58:7.
2. Isaiah 58:8–9.
3. See Joshua 1; Judges 1.
4. Joshua 14:12.
5. 1 Chronicles 4:10.

THE DREAM GIVER
RESOURCES

In order to serve you in your Quest for your Dream, visit the website

www.TheDreamGiver.com
www.brucewilkinson.com

or call toll-free

1-866-263-7822

for the following Dream Tools and other key information:

DailyDreams
Daily e-mail messages from the author of The Dream Giver

The Dream Assessment
Discover how your Personality affects your Dream

The Dream Journal
Capture your Dream while you Live it

The Dream Motivator
Inspiring quotes to keep you Dreaming

Music to Dream By
Music that inspires the Dream and the Dreamer

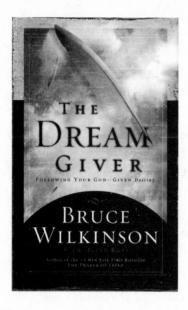